Quilt It with Love

The Project Linus Story

Quilt It with L❤ve

The Project Linus Story

20+ Quilt Patterns
& Stories to Warm Your Heart

Mary Balagna and Carol Babbitt

LARK CRAFTS
Asheville

EDITOR:
Amanda Carestio

COPY EDITOR:
Rebecca Behan

ART DIRECTORS:
Megan Kirby, Louise Walker,
and Shannon Yokeley

ILLUSTRATOR:
Orrin Lundgren

PHOTOGRAPHERS:
Steve Mann and S. Stills

COVER DESIGNER:
Louise Walker

LARK CRAFTS

An Imprint of Sterling Publishing
387 Park Avenue South
New York, NY 10016

If you have questions or comments about
this book, please visit: larkcrafts.com

Library of Congress Cataloging-in-Publication Data

Babbitt, Carol.
  Quilt it with love : the Project Linus story : 20+ quilt patterns and stories to warm your heart /
Carol Babbitt and Mary Balagna.
      pages cm
  Includes bibliographical references and index.
  ISBN 978-1-4547-0294-8 (alk. paper)
  1. Quilting--Patterns. 2. Children's quilts. 3. Project Linus--Anecdotes. I. Balagna, Mary. II. Title.
  TT835.B2125 2012
  746.46--dc23

                    2011047742

10 9 8 7 6 5 4 3 2

Published by Lark Crafts
An Imprint of Sterling Publishing Co., Inc.
387 Park Avenue South, New York, NY 10016

Text © 2012, Carol Babbitt and Mary Balagna
Photography © 2012, Lark Crafts, an Imprint of Sterling Publishing Co., Inc., unless otherwise specified
Illustrations © 2012, Lark Crafts, an Imprint of Sterling Publishing Co., Inc., except on page 9, ©2012
Peanuts Worldwide LLC

Distributed in Canada by Sterling Publishing,
c/o Canadian Manda Group, 165 Dufferin Street
Toronto, Ontario, Canada M6K 3H6

Distributed in the United Kingdom by GMC Distribution Services,
Castle Place, 166 High Street, Lewes, East Sussex, England BN7 1XU

Distributed in Australia by Capricorn Link (Australia) Pty Ltd.,
P.O. Box 704, Windsor, NSW 2756 Australia

Manufactured in China

ISBN 13: 978-1-4547-0294-8

For information about custom editions, special sales, and premium and corporate purchases, please
contact Sterling Special Sales Department at 800-805-5489 or specialsales@sterlingpub.com.

Requests for information about desk and examination copies available to college and university
professors must be submitted to academic@larkbooks.com. Our complete policy can be found
at www.larkcrafts.com.

This book is dedicated to our husbands, Kirk Babbitt and Terry Balagna, our children, our grandchildren, our Project Linus Coordinators, and our blanketeers who, in their own special way, offer comfort and security to children in need of a big hug.

Contents

The Quilts

welcome to
Quilt It with Love:
The Project Linus Story!

This book is the realization of a dream that began with a chance meeting in an elevator and evolved into a deep friendship and a rewarding working relationship. Now, along with hundreds of chapter coordinators and thousands of volunteers, we've become the Project Linus family.

How many times have you seen a heartbreaking story in the news or heard about a child faced with serious illness or trauma? Perhaps a family has come across hard times or lost a home in a fire or other disaster. Every day children across the United States face situations that cause enormous stress and anxiety. Physicians, hospitals, and medical personnel do what they can to treat the physical and mental needs of these children, but emotional support is sometimes not a priority. Parents and families are often traumatized as they watch their loved ones suffer. It is in these times that Project Linus can step in and bring comfort and security to children and to their families in the form of a handmade quilt or blanket.

Project ♥ Linus
Providing Security Through Blankets

Project Linus is a national non-profit organization, founded in 1995 with the mission to provide comfort, love, and a sense of security for children who are seriously ill, traumatized, or otherwise in need. It is also our mission to provide a fun and rewarding service opportunity for anyone who is interested in bringing a warm hug to a child. With nearly 400 chapters across the country and an estimated 60,000 volunteers, we have established relationships with hospitals, shelters, emergency response teams, schools, funeral homes, and countless other facilities to provide a little bit of comfort in scary and sometimes desperate situations. Handmade quilts and blankets of every kind are supplied to facilities every day. Volunteer Chapter Coordinators are constantly collecting and making blankets and seeking out children in their communities who are in need. With our help, medical staff now has the ability to wrap a warm blanket around the shoulders of an accident victim, or decorate the bed of a seriously ill child with a cheerful quilt, or protect a premature newborn from glaring lights. We've now donated these gifts to over 4 million children. And we have grown beyond our wildest dreams.

For years, we've dreamed of writing a book about our journey with Project Linus. We wanted to share the beautiful and touching stories we have heard and also some of the extraordinary examples of creativity and beauty that have been our pleasure to behold.

> *Project Linus is a national non-profit organization, founded in 1995 with the mission to provide comfort, love, and a sense of security for children who are seriously ill, traumatized, or otherwise in need.*

Within these pages, we've gathered together a collection of quilts perfect for making and giving. You'll find:

- ♥ Interactive quilts that move, delight, or double as a game board for a bed-bound child.

- ♥ Quilts with pockets for storing treats, tissue, or favorite toys.

- ♥ Cute quilts that stitch up quickly with strip piecing or make the most of fabric precuts.

- ♥ Quilts that are perfect for guild or group crafting projects.

From crazy quilting to appliqué to paper piecing, these quilts also represent a wide array of techniques and styles. We've included a Quilting Basics section, should you need a refresher on a particular technique.

We hope that you'll be inspired by these stories and patterns to become involved with Project Linus in your own communities. By purchasing this book, you've already made a contribution to Project Linus. If you would like to find out how to do more, please go to our website at www.projectlinus.org, and become a member of the Project Linus family.

Quilting Basics

Project Linus accepts blankets in all sizes and styles, including quilts, tied comforters, fleece blankets, and crocheted or knitted afghans in child-friendly colors. In a nutshell, blankets must be new, handmade, and washable. For the purposes of this book, we are featuring quilts in some of our favorite patterns that are simple and fun to make. We know that a handmade quilt is a treasure, and children understand that too. They know their Project Linus blanket was made by someone who was thinking of them, sending love in a handmade hug.

There are as many techniques and supplies available as there are quilters. It seems that everyone has their own favorite rotary cutter or thread, or their own tried-and-true technique for binding a quilt. Here's a list of items that we feel are essential to the Project Linus quilting enthusiast.

> ## BASIC SUPPLIES & TOOLS
> - Sewing machine
> - Scissors and seam ripper
> - Rotary cutter and mat
> - Hand sewing needles
> - Iron and ironing board
> - Embroidery tools and supplies
> - Fabric marking pencil
> - Safety and basting pins
> - Basic ruler set, including an angled ruler

Basic Supplies and Tools

Whether you are an accomplished quilter or a beginner, you'll find that that these tools and supplies will make your quilting experience more satisfying and successful. Many of these items are likely in your sewing kit now.

Fabric. Fabric is the most important element in your quilt, and it is not the place to skimp. Quality cotton fabrics that are marketed to quilters are the best choice, and they make an enormous difference to your finished project. There are many online choices for buying fabric but we recommend that you visit a local quilt shop if possible. There is nothing like browsing fabric bolts in person to get a feel for the fabric quality and how multiple fabrics mix and match.

Batting. Batting is available in many styles including cotton, polyester, wool, and mixed fibers. You can purchase them in precut sizes or off the bolt, and in various lofts (thickness or puffiness). We love cotton quilt batting with a low loft. This type of batting is the easiest to place and to quilt, producing a beautiful and cozy end result.

Rotary Cutter. Rotary cutters are available in several sizes from 18mm to 60mm in diameter. A 45mm rotary cutter is a great midsize cutter that you can use for most projects. Choose one with a handle that fits comfortably in your hand.

Rotary Cutting Mat. Choose the largest mat you can afford that fits your work area. It should have a grid for easy fabric placement and measurement.

Ruler. These are not your everyday rulers, but special acrylic clear rulers marked with thin grid lines. There are so many ruler shapes and sizes on the market now that you can easily get overwhelmed. Choose a few basic sizes to get started. We recommend quilters invest in rulers that measure 6 x 12 inches (15.2 x 30 cm), 6 x 24 inches (15.2 x 61 cm), and 6½ inches (16.5 cm) square.

Pins. Pins are essential for securing layers. Choose good, long, thin, rustproof pins made especially for quilting. We love the flower-head pins because they are easy to handle, they don't add bulk, and you can iron right over them.

Freezer Paper. Freezer paper, which can be found at the grocery store in the paper aisle, is used for stabilizing fabric so that it can be embellished with drawings or signatures. Cut a piece of freezer paper the same size as your fabric piece. Using an iron on a medium setting, adhere the fabric (wrong side) to the freezer paper (shiny side). Press until the fabric feels stiff. You can now use fabric markers to decorate the fabric with ease. Remove the freezer paper and reuse in the same manner.

Seam Ripper. A seam ripper is your saving grace. Every quilter needs one.

Scissors. You'll need two good pairs of scissors: one that you use exclusively for fabric and one that you can use for cutting paper templates and other materials.

Thread. Make sure you have 100 percent cotton thread in white, off white, gray, and black. If you are machine quilting, you may want to match colors with your fabric, but otherwise the basic colors work just fine.

Glue Sticks. Everyday school glue sticks, found in any office supply store, are used to temporarily affix fabric to paper when using the Foundation Paper Piecing technique.

Basic Techniques

It is easy to be overwhelmed by the multitude of techniques and terms in quilting. With experience, you'll become familiar with them and determine which ones work for your style and your project. Accuracy and precision are key to making a great quilt, so we've included a few of the fundamentals to help you make the perfect Project Linus quilt.

Pressing

Pressing instructions are usually included in the individual project. Seams must be pressed according to directions in order to minimize bulk and to allow for ease of matching seams. You don't need a fancy iron; an inexpensive iron works beautifully. Use the appropriate temperature for the fabric you are using, and apply gentle pressure.

Appliqué

Appliqué is a basic process that entails applying small pieces of fabric onto a larger background with a variety of techniques. You will find many tutorials online for varying techniques including needle-turn appliqué, freezer paper appliqué, and more. Any will work beautifully for the appliqué patterns in this book.

For most of the quilts in this book, we chose to use raw-edge appliqué with paper-backed fusible webbing. To do this, you will need to trace the appliqué design in reverse onto the paper backing. Fuse the webbing to the wrong side of the fabric. Cut out your design along the traced lines, cutting fabric and webbing layers all together. Peel off the remaining paper leaving the webbing on the fabric. Place your shape as desired on the background fabric. Press for 10 to 15 seconds until secure. Be sure to refer to the manufacturer's instructions for the fusible webbing that you choose. If desired, finish the edges with a hand or machine stitch to secure the edges even further.

♥ WOF=WIDTH OF FABRIC
What is meant by WOF? This is a term you will see throughout this book. WOF stands for width of fabric and indicates the measurement from selvage to selvage. Most quilting fabrics are between 42 inches (106.7 cm) and 44 inches (111.8 cm) wide. So, for example if you are asked to cut 4-inch (10.2 cm) x WOF strips, you would cut a strip from selvage to selvage that measures 4 inches (10.2 cm) wide.

♥ TO WASH OR NOT TO WASH?
There are many different answers to this one simple question: should fabric be washed before quilting? Fabric comes from the manufacturer with chemicals applied to the surface that give it a crisp feel and appearance. Some quilters like the feel and appearance of the fabric "as is," and some believe that you must always launder the fabric before use. No matter where you side on the issue, here are some factors to consider:

Cotton fabrics will shrink, usually with the first washing, but all fabrics do not shrink at the same rate. (Many quilters like the effect this gives a quilt, and others see the puckers as ruinous!)

Some colors will run. If you are using deep reds or other intense colors, the dye could run and bleed onto lighter colors when washed. You don't want this to happen after your quilt is constructed.

Chemicals. It's a good idea to prewash fabrics if you are making quilts for children, especially children who are ill or who may have compromised respiratory systems.

Foundation Paper Piecing

Foundation paper piecing consists of sewing pieces of fabric onto a paper foundation to form a quilt block. This piecing technique allows a quilter to construct complicated patterns easily and accurately, and it's a very good way to use up small scraps of fabric. Each template pattern that requires foundation paper piecing will give you a suggested enlargement percentage as well as a numeric order that you should work in.

1 Dab glue in the center of fabric piece #1 and place piece #1, centered and right side up, on the *unprinted side* of the paper foundation pattern. Using a light board will help you to position the fabric accurately over the area to be covered. Make sure that you've covered foundation piece #1 with at least a ¼-inch (6 mm) overhang on all sides (**Fig. 1**).

2 Place fabric piece #2 over piece #1 on the wrong side of the foundation square with right sides together (**Fig. 2**). If the piece is large, you may want to place two pins on the edge most distant to the sewing line (this will keep you from sewing over pins) to secure the piece in place.

3 Carefully turn the foundation paper over so the marked side of the paper is facing you, taking care not to disturb either fabric piece that has just been placed. Sew on the printed line that divides piece #1 and piece #2 (**Fig. 3**).

Note: Use a small stitch length. This will help to perforate the foundation paper and facilitate easy removal.

4 Perform a quick check that this piece has been properly placed by holding the foundation paper up to a light source. Foundation piece #1 should be totally covered by this new piece of fabric with at least ¼ inch (6 mm) extra on all sides. If it isn't,

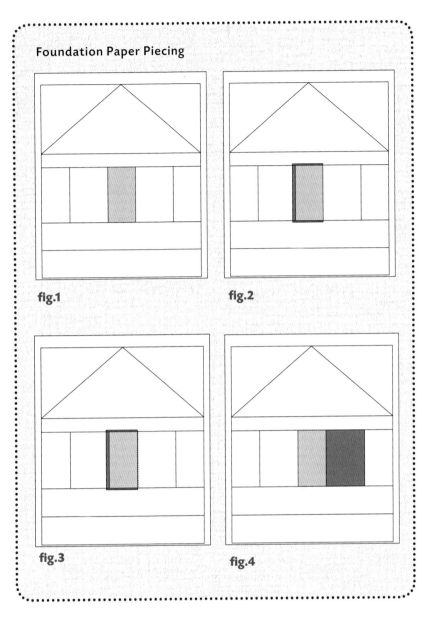

Foundation Paper Piecing

fig.1

fig.2

fig.3

fig.4

remove the stitching and reposition the fabric, then resew the seam. Press in position.

5 Place the block on a rotary cutting mat with the printed side of the foundation block facing upwards. Fold the foundation paper on the seam line (use a postcard or ruler as a guide) just sewn so that the printed sides of that paper are facing each other and the seam allowance of fabric piece #1 and fabric piece #2 is exposed. Trim the seam allowance to ¼ inch (6 mm). A rotary cutter will make this step much easier.

6 Unfold the foundation paper, and press fabric piece #2 into position (**Fig.4**). While finger pressing will work, pressing with an iron will produce a more accurate block and also flattens the fold line in the foundation paper.

7 Repeat for the rest of the pieces. Trim the block to the edge of foundation pattern (which includes a ¼-inch [6 mm] seam allowance).

8 Press and carefully remove the paper backing.

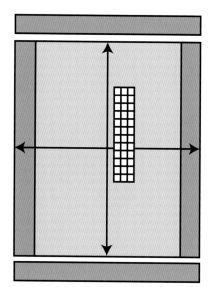

Fig. 5: Adding a straight border

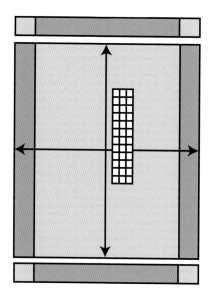

Fig. 6: Adding a border with corners

Adding Borders

Borders can be cut in one seamless strip or can be pieced. When piecing borders, the most efficient way to use your fabric is to cut a strip across the width of the fabric. If the length of the border needed is longer than 40 to 42 inches (101.6 to 106.7 cm), cut more than one strip and piece them together. We've included instructions for three common border techniques that adapt perfectly for almost any quilt.

Note: It is most important to measure and cut border strips to fit your quilt, rather than simply sewing a fabric strip to the edge of the quilt top and then trimming to size. Cutting the strips and sewing them to the quilt top without measuring can produce a wavy and uneven border.

Adding a Straight Border (Fig. 5)

1 Measure the length of the quilt top through the vertical center. This will be the length of the vertical border strips. Mark the centers of the border strips. If borders need to be pieced, sew two of the 40 to 42-inch (101.6 to 106.7 cm) strips together, and then cut them to the measured length of the quilt top.

2 Pin the borders to the sides of the quilt top, matching the border's center mark with the center of the side of the quilt. Match up the ends of the border to the edges of the quilt top, and then ease in and pin as needed. Sew in place with a ¼-inch (6 mm) seam. Press seams toward the border strips.

3 Measure the width of the quilt top through the horizontal center, including the vertical borders that were just sewn to the quilt top. Cut horizontal border strips to that measurement and mark, pin, and stitch as in step 2.

4 Press the seams toward the border strips.

Adding a Border with Corner Squares (Fig. 6)

1 Measure the length and width of the quilt top through the center. This will be the length of the vertical and horizontal border strips without corner squares. Mark the centers of the border strips. If necessary, piece border strips together to the needed dimensions.

2 Pin the vertical borders to the sides of the quilt top, matching the border's center mark with the center of the side of the quilt. Match up the ends of the border to the edges of the quilt top, and then ease in and pin as needed. Sew in place with a ¼-inch (6 mm) seam.

3 Sew a corner square to each end of the remaining (horizontal) border strips, and press the seams toward the border strip.

4 Pin the borders to the top and bottom edges of the quilt top, matching the centers and ends, and ease in as necessary. Pin and then sew in place with a ¼-inch (6 mm) seam.

5 Press the seams toward the border.

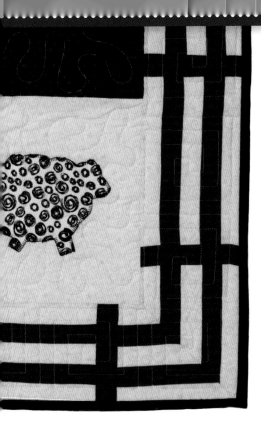

Adding a Border with a Mitered Corner (Fig. 7)

1 To calculate the length of the top and bottom border strips needed, double the width of the border and add that measurement to the width of the quilt top edge, plus 2 inches (5.1 cm). For example, if your border is 3½ inches (8.9 cm) wide and your quilt top horizontal edge measures 36 inches (91.4 cm), you will add 9 inches (22.9 cm) to the 36 inches (91.4 cm), meaning you'll need to cut strips that are 45 inches (109.2 cm) long.

2 In the same manner, determine the side border length by doubling the border width and then adding that measurement to the length of the quilt top vertical edges, and add 2 inches (5.1 cm). Cut two strips of border fabric to this size.

3 Starting with the top border, center the border fabric to the quilt. Use pins to hold the border, and stitch the border, in place with a ¼-inch (6 mm) seam allowance. Stop sewing ¼ inch (6 mm) from the edge of the quilt top, and backstitch or lockstitch to keep the thread from unraveling. Repeat this method with the bottom border, and then the two side borders. Iron the seams toward the border.

4 Place the quilt top right side up on the ironing board. Fold the end of the border back so that it rests on top of itself with the right sides touching. Using an angled ruler, adjust the border until you achieve a 45° angle at the quilt top's corner. Repeat for the border fabric that is also touching this corner. Press with the iron to make a crease.

5 Fold the entire quilt at an angle with the right sides together. Align the border fabric raw edges and the border seams along with the crease marks. Stitch along the crease mark, and backstitch to lock the stitch line in place.

Note: If the ironed crease is difficult to see, you can draw a line on the crease with a fabric marking pencil.

6 Trim the excess fabric way from the stitch line to leave a ¼-inch (6 mm) seam allowance. Press the mitered seam open with the iron. Press the mitered seam open and repeat steps 4 and 5 for all corners.

CREATING THE BACKING
Pieced or plain, you'll need some kind of backing for your quilt. If your quilt measures less than about 44 inches (111.8 cm) in width, it's easy to make a single piece backing using one piece of fabric which is normally about 45 inches (114.3 cm) wide. However, if your quilt top is wider than 44 inches (111.8 cm), you'll need to make a horizontally pieced backing. You can piece it with either two or three pieces. If the quilt's vertical measurement is 80 inches (203.2 cm) or less, you can horizontally piece the backing with two pieces. If it is larger, you will need to use three pieces, but the process is the same.

Take the horizontal measurement of the quilt. Add 4 inches (10.2 cm) to that measurement and cut two pieces of fabric to the calculated size. Cut off the selvage edges and, right sides together, sew the two pieces together creating a quilt backing with the seam running horizontally across the quilt. Press seams to one side.

Take the vertical measurement of the quilt and add 4 inches (10.2 cm) to that measurement. Trim the backing to the calculated size, cutting an equal amount of fabric off the top and the bottom edge of the backing.

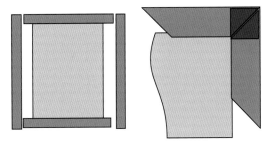
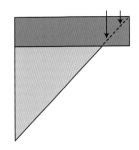
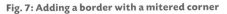

Fig. 7: Adding a border with a mitered corner

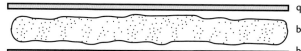

quilt top (right side up)

batting

backing (right side down)

Fig. 8

Free-Motion Quilting

Finishing the Quilt

Now that your quilt top is completed, it is time to layer it with a backing and batting to create your quilt "sandwich."

Stacking the Layers

A common technique for securing your layers before quilting is pin basting. On a large surface, such as a table or the floor, lay your backing fabric down, right side down and smooth. Next layer the batting over the backing fabric and then your quilt top, right side up **(Fig. 8)**. Smooth all of your layers. Beginning in the middle of the quilt, pin the layers together using safety or basting pins. Smooth as you go, and continue pinning until the entire quilt is secure.

Quilting

You have three basic options when it comes to quilting your project.

Machine Quilting

Machine quilting can be accomplished on a long-arm quilting machine or on your everyday home sewing machine with a few simple adjustments.

Straight Stitching: For straight stitching, you will be quilting in a gridded pattern that you mark on the quilt or one that you can see within the pattern that is pieced. Be sure to use a walking foot on your home machine. This will enable the machine to pull all the layers through at the same rate.

Free-Motion Quilting: For free-motion quilting, you'll need to use a special free-motion foot or a darning foot. The most basic kind of free-motion quilting is done in a fluid loopy design called stippling, beginning in the center of the quilt and working outward. Be sure to follow the instructions included with your machine.

Hand Quilting

Hand quilting can be done in a number of ways. You can stabilize the quilt in a hoop, in a quilt frame, or hold it on your lap. Using a quilting needle and cotton thread, knot the end of the thread. Insert your needle into the desired location on your quilt from the top layer, into the batting and then back up without going through the back of the quilt. Gently "pop" the knot into the middle of the quilt and into the batting. Use a running stitch along your desired quilting lines, keeping the stitches even and small—about six or seven per inch (2.5 cm).

Tying

An easy—and quick!—way to sew your quilt together is to tie it. This is done using a sharp needle with a large eye and perle cotton thread. Using a long length of thread, stitch down and back up through all the layers without making a knot. For best results, make sure your stitch is about ⅛ to ¼ inch (3 to 6 mm) wide and no larger. Continue with these stitches about every 3 or 4 inches (7.6 to 10.2 cm) in a grid pattern. When you have stitched the entire quilt, cut the thread between the stitches and tie in a square knot. Trim the tails to 1 inch (2.5 cm).

Binding

Your binding is the final step in constructing your quilt. The principle is quite simple: you're basically applying a strip of fabric over the raw edges of the quilt. Quilt bindings provide that final flourish—plus added durability—for your quilt. These instructions include information for making your own binding strips. If you're planning to use store-bought binding, skip to step 7.

1 Prepare the quilt for binding by trimming the edges using a rotary cutter, ruler, and mat so that the quilt top, batting, and backing are aligned.

2 Measure the perimeter of the quilt. For example, if your finished quilt is 45 x 60 inches (114.3 x 152.4 cm), the perimeter will measure 210 inches (533.4 cm). Add 12 inches (30.5 cm) to this measurement to get the total needed binding.

3 For a ½-inch (1.3 cm) finished binding, cut fabric strips 2½ inches (6.4 cm) by the width of the fabric. For a binding of 222 inches (563.9 cm), you will need to cut approximately five strips.

4 Join the strips together end to end with a mitered seam. To do this, lay two strip ends perpendicular to each other, right sides together. Using a ruler with a 45° marking, mark a diagonal line across the corner. Stitch across this line and trim seam to ¼ inch (6 mm) **(Fig. 9)**. Press to one side.

5 Repeat for all strips until you have one continuous strip of fabric.

6 Fold the entire length of the strip in half lengthwise, wrong sides together and press.

7 Starting in the middle of one side of the quilt on the front, align the binding along the edge, raw edges together.

8 Fold the beginning end of the binding at a 45° angle and press.

9 Leaving a binding "tail" of about 8 inches (20.3 cm), begin stitching the binding to the quilt edge. Use a scant ½-inch (1.3 cm) seam allowance to allow for turning.

10 At the corner, stop stitching when you get to the equal distance for the seam allowance. Backstitch to lock the seams in place, and remove the quilt from the sewing machine.

11 Fold the binding back on itself perpendicular to the last seam **(Fig. 10)**. Then fold the binding again, bringing it back toward you. The fold will align with the raw edge you just sewed. Line up the raw edges of the binding with the next edge of the quilt.

12 Begin at the edge of the quilt and stitch the binding to the second side of the quilt. Continue to attach the binding, repeating the above steps for each corner.

13 When you come back to the beginning side, stitch the binding as before but stop about 10 inches (25.4 cm) from the end/beginning.

14 Unfold the end section of the binding fabric and align along the edge of the quilt. Layer the beginning mitered end over the ending binding and smooth. Mark the ending binding along the 45° angle.

15 With the right sides of the binding together, line up the marked angle with the folded angle and stitch along

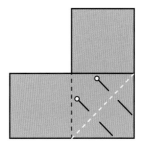

Fig. 9

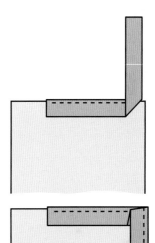

Fig. 10

the line. Refold the binding and lay in place to assure you have measured correctly. If it lies flat, trip the binding seam to ¼ inch (6 mm).

16 Refold the binding and align with the edge of the quilt. Stitch the remaining edge of the binding to the quilt as before.

17 Fold the binding over the raw edges of the quilt, making sure to cover the binding seam. Hand stitch in place, or machine stitch from the top.

Designed by Caroline Embleton

Pieced by Mary Balagna   Quilted by Ron and Kay Gerard

Come Sail Away

You're the captain of this Project Linus ship. From a stack of squares, you can create a sailboat unlike any other.

FINISHED QUILT SIZE
36½" x 50" (92.7 x 127 cm)

FINISHED BLOCK SIZE
7½" square (19 cm)

SEAM ALLOWANCE
¼" (6 mm)

MATERIALS
Basic Supplies & Tools, page 11

- **Sky:** ½ yard (.5 m) of fabric
- **Sail #1:** Scrap fabric, at least 8¾" square (22.2 cm)
- **Sail #2:** Scrap fabric, at least 8¾" square (22.2 cm)
- **Boat:** ¼ yard (.2 m) of fabric
- **Water:** ¼ yard (.2 m) of fabric
- **Border:** ¾ yard (.7 m) of fabric
- **Backing:** 1¾ yards (1.6 m) of backing fabric
- **Binding:** ½ yard (.5 m) of binding fabric
- **Batting:** 40" x 55" (101.6 x 139.7 cm)

DIFFICULTY

Cutting

From sky fabric:
Cut one strip, 8" (20.3 cm) x WOF (width of fabric), and one strip 8¾" (22.2 cm) x WOF

Cut the 8" (20.3 cm) strip into five 8" (20.3 cm) squares.

Cut the 8¾" (22.2 cm) strip into two 8¾" (22.2 cm) squares and three 8" (20.3 cm) squares.

From sail fabrics:
Cut one 8¾" (22.2 cm) square from each fabric.

From boat fabric:
Cut one strip, 8¾" (22.2 cm) x WOF.

Cut the 8¾" (22.2 cm) strip into one 8¾" (22.2 cm) square and two 8" (20.3 cm) squares.

From water fabric:
Cut one strip, 8¾" (22.2 cm) x WOF.

Cut the 8¾" (22.2 cm) strip into one 8¾" (22.2 cm) square and four 8" (20.3 cm) squares.

From border fabric:
Cut two strips, 3½" (8.9 cm) x WOF.

Cut two strips, 6½" (16.5 cm) x WOF.

From binding fabric:
Cut fabric into five strips, 2½" (6.4 cm) x WOF.

Dear Project Linus,

My son and I wanted to thank you so much for a blanket given to him by his school guidance counselor. Just days before this school year started, his aunt, who had long been suffering from cancer, passed away. On several different occasions, something happened at school to remind him of his aunt's death, and as his hospice counselor has suggested, the fact that I am ill (though not terminally so) worries him greatly. Combine that with worry about his youngest cousin, and this very sensitive little guy found himself overwhelmed by emotion. He went to the school library one day and asked for help in finding books about cancer. He began to cry, remembering his aunt.

A teacher took him to the guidance counselor, who talked to him about cancer and gave him one of your wonderful blankets. Special permission was granted for him to carry the blanket to school every day in his backpack. The blanket also comes home with him every day, and he sleeps with it every night now.

I can't tell you the comfort your blanket has given my son during a very difficult time. He feels so special not only that he was given such a warm, fuzzy, feel-good thing, but that someone unknown to him cares about children enough to have made the blanket. He's so proud of his blanket! When he first brought the blanket home and I found the tag on it, I myself got a little teary-eyed. I found your website, and I had a really good cry reading about all of the projects going on and the letters from others about your blankets. Recent world events, and personal ones, have made me question the very nature of humanity lately. The gift of one of your blankets to my son has helped to restore my faith in the goodness of human nature. I hope every blanketeer realizes it is never "just a blanket." The comfort you have provided in a time of sorrow will not be forgotten.

With heartfelt thanks,
A mom and a son

Assembly

Creating the Blocks

1 Stack a large sky square and the sail fabric #1 square, right sides together, and draw a pencil line diagonally from corner to corner. Sew on each side of the line, using a ¼-inch (6 mm) seam allowance. Cut along the pencil line and press open. Trim the square to 8 inches (20.3 cm) **(Fig. 1)**.

2 Repeat step 1 with the remaining large sky square and the sail fabric #2 square.

3 Repeat step 1 with the large water square and the large boat square.

Assembling the Quilt Top

4 Piece together the sky, sail, boat, and water blocks, referring to the sample photograph.

Adding Borders

5 Add borders as follows (page 14): Sew the thin border strips to the side edges and the thick border strips to the top and bottom edges of the quilt.

Finishing the Quilt

6 Create the backing, following the instructions on page 15. Layer the backing, batting, and quilt top to make a quilt sandwich and baste the layers together.

7 Quilt as desired.

8 Sew the binding strips together and bind the edge of the quilt, following the Binding instructions, page 17.

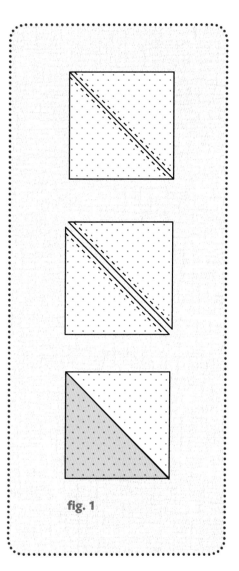

fig. 1

Ask your online knitting, crocheting, or quilting groups to donate blanket-making materials to your local Project Linus chapter.

Designed by Judy Brumaster

Pieced by Mary Balagna   Quilted by Linda Kirby

x

♥ 22 ♥   quilt it with love

Happy Hearts

*Small hearts, medium hearts, and large hearts—we've filled
this beautiful quilt with plenty of happiness and love.*

FINISHED QUILT SIZE
47" x 60" (119.4 x 152.4 cm)

FINISHED BLOCK SIZE
12" square (30.5 cm)

SEAM ALLOWANCE
¼" (6 mm)

MATERIALS
- Basic Supplies & Tools, page 11
- **Pink heart fabrics:** ½ yard (.5 m)
  each of coordinating light and dark
  pink fabrics
- **Blue heart fabrics:** ½ yard (.5 m)
  each of coordinating light and dark
  blue fabrics
- **Background, sashing, inner
  border fabric:** 1½ yards (1.4 m) of
  white fabric
- **Border:** 1¾ yards (1.6 m) of print
  fabric (or ¾ yard [.7 m] for
  pieced border)
- **Backing:** 2¾ yards (2.5 m) of
  backing fabric
- **Binding:** ½ yard (.5 m) of
  binding fabric
- **Batting:** 51" x 64"
  (129.5 x 162.6 cm)

Cutting
**From dark pink and light
blue heart fabrics:**
Cut one strip, 6½" (16.5 cm) x WOF
(width of fabric), from each fabric.

Cut one strip, 7" (17.8 cm) x WOF,
from each fabric.

Cut each of the 6½" (16.5 cm) strips
into six 6½" (16.5 cm) squares.

Cut each of the 7" (17.8 cm) strips
into four 7" (17.8 cm) squares.

Cut two of the 7" (17.8 cm)
squares of each fabric into eight
3½" (8.9 cm) squares.

Trim the remaining 7" (17.8 cm)
squares to measure 6½" square
(16.5 cm).

**From light pink and dark blue
heart fabrics:**
Cut one strip, 8" (20.3 cm) x WOF,
from each fabric.

Cut each strip into five 8"
(20.3 cm) squares.

Cut one square of each fabric into
four 4" (10.2 cm) squares.

Trim four 8" (20.3 cm) squares of
each fabric into 7" (17.8 cm) squares.

From white background fabric:
Cut thirty-two 2½" (6.4 cm) squares
for large hearts.

Cut thirty-two 1¼" (3.2 cm) squares
for small hearts.

Cut eight 7" (17.8 cm) squares for
large hearts.

Cut eight 4" (10.2 cm) squares for
small hearts.

Cut eight 6½" (16.5 cm) squares
for small hearts.

Cut eight strips, 1½" x 12½"
(3.8 x 31.8 cm), for vertical sashing.

Cut five strips, 1½" x 38½" (3.8 x
97.9 cm), for horizontal sashing.

Cut four strips, 1½" (3.8 cm) x WOF,
for vertical inner border.

From outer border fabric:
Cut four strips, 4" (10.2 cm) x LOF
(length of fabric).

From binding fabric:
Cut six strips, 2" (6.4 cm) x WOF.

DIFFICULTY 🖤 🖤

Hi, Project Linus.
*My name is Sarah, and I was a sopho-
more at Columbine High School when the
tragic massacre occurred. During the next
few days, the only thing we found bear-
able was being with our friends and those
who had been with us on that horrible
day. Our church was holding a service
project for Project Linus and many of the
women gathered at the church to make
blankets, tie them, and send them off.
My friends and sister and I found this
to be the best sort of therapy. We were
able to put aside our worries and fears
for those few days and while we made
blankets together and thought about the
many children that would be blessed by
the service of those women.*

*   I just thought I would share this story
with you. It is something that I will never
forget. It was a way for us to have hope
at a time when hope seemed to be lost.*

*   Thank you for the wonderful gift.*
*   Sarah*

Assembly

Creating the Large Heart Blocks

1 Draw a pencil line diagonally from corner to corner on the wrong side of four 2½-inch (6.4 cm) white background squares. Place one square in each upper corner of a 6½-inch (16.5 cm) dark pink square and a light blue square. Stitch along the marked lines as shown **(Fig. 1)**.

2 Trim the seam allowances to ¼ inch (6 mm). Discard the corner pieces **(Fig. 2)**. Press the seam allowances toward the darker fabric.

3 Sew the pieced squares together, creating the top half of the Large Heart Block **(Fig. 3)**.

4 Repeat steps 1–3 to create eight total top halves of the Large Heart Blocks. Press the pieces toward the dark pink fabric.

5 Stack a 7-inch (17.8 cm) white background square and a light pink square, right sides together. Draw a pencil line diagonally from corner to corner on the white square. Sew ¼ inch (6 mm) from each side of the marked line. Cut along the line, creating two white/light pink blocks **(Fig. 4)**. Press the seams toward the white fabric.

6 Repeat step 5 using a 7-inch (17.8 cm) white background square and dark blue square. Press the seams toward the dark blue fabric.

7 Piece together a white/dark blue block and a white/light pink block, creating the lower half of the Large Heart Block **(Fig. 5)**.

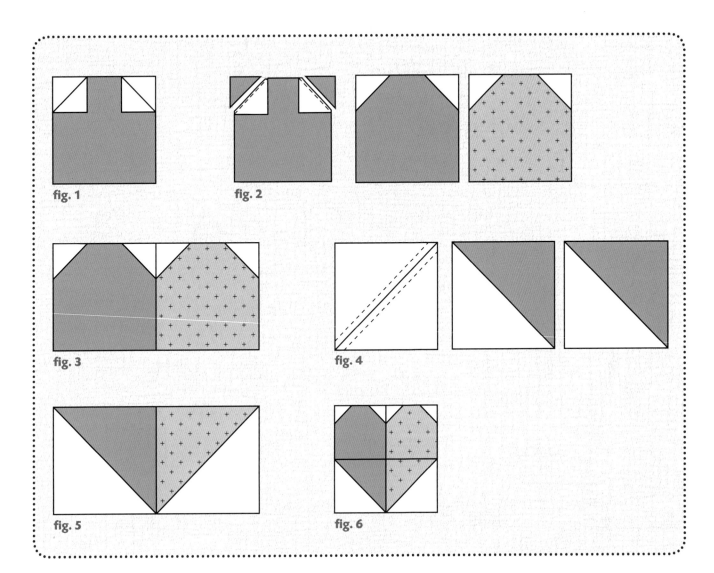

fig. 1

fig. 2

fig. 3

fig. 4

fig. 5

fig. 6

8 Repeat steps 5–7 to create eight total lower halves of the Large Heart Blocks. Press the pieces toward dark blue fabric.

9 Piece together each Large Heart Block, joining a top and bottom half. Press the center seams toward the top half of each heart block—eight total Large Heart Blocks (**Fig. 6**).

Project Linus's mission is to provide love, a sense of security, warmth, and comfort to children who are seriously ill, traumatized, or otherwise in need through the gifts of new, handmade blankets and afghans, lovingly created by volunteer "blanketeers."

Creating the Small Heart Blocks

10 Follow the instructions for creating the Large Heart Blocks, substituting the pieces as follows—eight total Small Heart Blocks:

- Substitute 1¼-inch (3.2 cm) white background squares for the 2½-inch (6.4 cm) white background squares.

- Substitute 3½-inch (8.9 cm) dark pink and light blue squares for the 6½-inch (16.5 cm) dark pink and light blue squares.

- Substitute 4-inch (10.2 cm) light pink and dark blue squares for the 7-inch (17.8 cm) light pink and dark blue squares.

- Substitute 4-inch (10.2 cm) white background squares for the 7-inch (17.8 cm) white background squares.

11 Stitch together a 6½-inch (16.5 cm) background square to one side of a Small Heart Block. Press toward the background square. Repeat to create four total rectangles with the background square on the left of the heart block and four with the background square on the right.

12 Join the rectangles together in pairs as shown, creating four total 12½-inch (31.8 cm) blocks (**Fig. 7**).

Assembling the Quilt Top

13 Join together the blocks and the vertical sashing strips as shown in the sample photograph to create four rows of three blocks each (**Fig. 8**).

14 Join the four rows together with the horizontal sashing strips, sewing the strips above and below each row.

Note: *Always measure the size of the finished blocks and adjust the length of the sashing strips accordingly, as needed.*

15 Sew an inner border strip to the top and bottom of the quilt top. Sew the remaining inner border strips to the vertical sides.

16 Add the outer borders to the quilt top, following the Adding a Border with a Mitered Corner instructions, page 15.

Finishing the Quilt

17 Create the backing, following the instructions on page 15. Layer the backing, batting, and quilt top to make a quilt sandwich and baste the layers together.

18 Quilt as desired.

19 Sew the binding strips together and bind the edge of the quilt, following the Binding instructions, page 17.

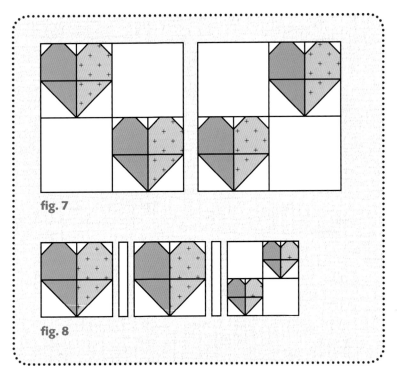

fig. 7

fig. 8

Designed by Elzora Channer

Pieced and quilted by Mary Balagna

Channer's Checkers

A fun game and a source of comfort, this quilt doubles as a checkerboard, with hidden pockets for the checkers.

FINISHED QUILT SIZE
42" x 60" (106.7 x 152.4 cm)

SEAM ALLOWANCE
¼" (6 mm)

MATERIALS
Basic Supplies & Tools, page 11

- Checker Template, page 123
- Pocket Template, page 123
- Checkerboard, pockets, and borders fabric A: 1¼ yards (1.1 m) of fabric
- Checkerboard, pockets, and borders fabric B: 1¼ yards (1.1 m) of fabric
- Inner border fabric C: ½ yard (.5 m)
- Checkers: Two 9" x 12" (22.9 x 30.5 cm) felt sheets in coordinating colors
- Backing: 1¾ yards (1.6 m) of backing fabric
- **Binding:** ½ yard (.5 m) of binding fabric
- **Batting:** 46 x 64" (116.8 x 162.6 cm)

Cutting

From checkerboard fabric A:
Cut 12 strips, 3½" (8.9 cm) x WOF (width of fabric).

From checkerboard fabric B:
Cut 11 strips, 3½" (8.9 cm) x WOF.

From inner border fabric C:
Cut four strips, 3½" (8.9 cm) x WOF.

From binding fabric:
Cut six strips, 2½" (6.4 cm) x WOF.

From checkers felt:
Photocopy or trace the Checker Template on page 123. Using the template, cut 12 circles from each felt sheet—24 checkers.

DIFFICULTY

Assembly
Creating the Blocks

1 Sew eight fabric A strips to eight fabric B strips in pairs, making eight A/B strip sets. Press the seams toward the darker fabric.

2 Sew together two sets of A/B strips, making four A/B-A/B strip sets (**Fig. 1**). Press the seams toward the darker fabric.

Dear Project Linus,

I want to thank you so much for the beautiful blanket my three-year-old son received from your organization while in the Pediatric Intensive Unit. Chase was hit by a car. He had just been taken off life support and was breathing on his own. He was very scared. That's when his nurse, Kim, came in with a Project Linus blanket. He had the blanket with him throughout his stay in the hospital and now uses it at home. Occasionally he will share it with his two brothers. Project Linus is a great idea and such a wonderful thing to do for sick and injured children. I know I am so very grateful for what strangers did for my precious son during such a scary and unsure time. He was comforted by his blanket and that comforted me! Our family would be happy to do anything we can to help with this project so please let us know what we can do. God bless you all. Thanks again.

3 Cut two A/B-A/B strip sets, as shown, into eight 3½-inch-wide (8.9 cm) rectangles—16 total rectangles (**Fig. 1**). Set aside the leftover scrap from each strip set for the pockets.

4 Piece together four 16-patch blocks. Join the blocks to make the checkerboard portion of the quilt—64 total squares (**Fig. 2**).

Assembling the Quilt Top

5 Add the inner border as follows: Sew a fabric C strip to each side edge of the checkerboard. Then sew the remaining inner border strips to the top and bottom edges of the checkerboard.

6 Add the next set of borders in the same way, sewing a fabric A strip to each side edge, and then sewing fabric A strips to the top and bottom edges.

7 Sew an A/B-A/B strip set to the top and bottom edges of the quilt, joining a fabric B strip to the fabric A border.

8 Cut one fabric B strip in half widthwise and sew each half to the remaining full-length fabric B strips, making two long strips for the vertical borders. Sew a border to each side of the quilt.

> *Project Linus donates blankets to children, infants through teens. Many sizes are appropriate depending on chapter need.*

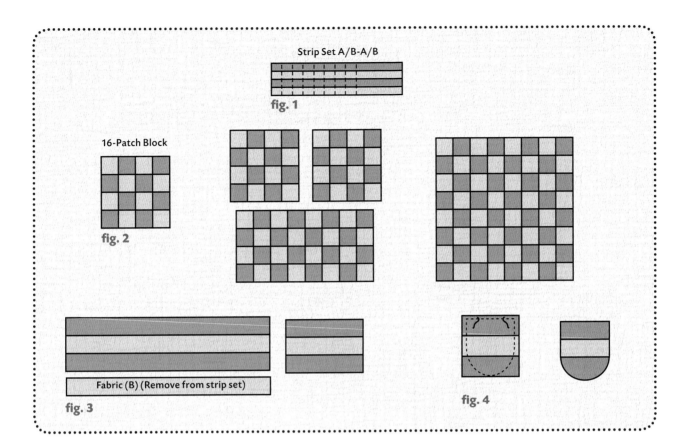

Strip Set A/B-A/B

fig. 1

16-Patch Block

fig. 2

Fabric (B) (Remove from strip set)

fig. 3

fig. 4

Creating the Pockets

9 Remove a fabric B strip from each leftover A/B-A/B strip set aside in step 3 **(Fig. 3)**. Cut two rectangles from the remaining portion of the strip sets, 13½ x 9½ inches (34.3 x 24.1 cm).

10 Fold the rectangles in half width-wise, right sides together, and stitch closed the vertical edge to make a tube. Center the seams in the back and press the tubes flat with the seams open. Do not turn the tubes right side out.

11 Photocopy or trace the Pocket Template on page 123. Mark and trim each tube shape using the template, and stitch closed as shown, leaving an opening to turn. Clip the corners and the rounded edges, turn, and then stitch the opening closed **(Fig. 4)**.

12 Position the pockets on the quilt top as desired and topstitch in place, leaving the top pocket edges open to hold checkers. Secure the top edges of the pockets by backstitching at the beginning and ending of the stitches. Place checkers in the pockets.

Finishing the Quilt

13 Create the backing, following the instructions on page 15. Layer the backing, batting, and quilt top to make a quilt sandwich and baste the layers together.

14 Quilt as desired.

15 Sew the binding strips together and bind the edge of the quilt, following the Binding instructions, page 17.

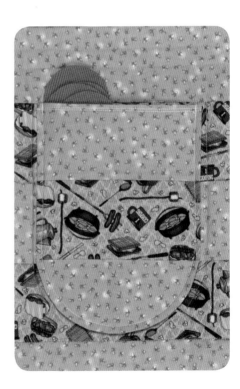

Designed by Cari Balagna Shields

Pieced and quilted by Mary Balagna

Lift Where You Stand

These barbell blocks serve as a reminder that we all have the strength and the power to overcome any adversity that we face.

FINISHED QUILT SIZE
46" x 62½" (116.8 x 158.8 cm)

FINISHED BLOCK SIZE
8" square (20.3 cm)

SEAM ALLOWANCE
¼" (6 mm)

MATERIALS
- Basic Supplies & Tools, page 11
- **Barbell blocks:** 9 fat quarters (45.7 x 55.9 cm) of solid fabric in assorted colors
- **Background fabric, inner border, outer border, corner squares:** 2 yards (1.8 m) of fabric
- **Contrasting border:** ⅓ yard (.3 m) of contrasting fabric
- **Backing:** 3 yards (2.7 m) of backing fabric
- **Binding:** ½ yard (.5 m) of binding fabric
- **Batting:** 50" x 66" (127 x 167.6 cm)

Notes: To make 24 identical barbell blocks you will need 1 yard (.9 m) of barbell fabric, cut into forty-eight 4½" squares (11.4 cm) and forty-eight 2½" squares (6.4 cm). Backing for this quilt must be horizontally pieced.

DIFFICULTY

Cutting

From the barbell fabrics:
Cut 4½" (11.4 cm) squares and 2½" (6.4 cm) squares as follows:

Dark red (color #1):
two squares each size.

Red (color #2):
four squares each size.

Orange (color #3):
six squares each size.

Yellow (color #4):
eight squares each size.

Light green (color #5):
eight squares each size.

Green (color #6):
eight squares each size.

Blue (color #7): six squares each size.

Purple (color #8):
four squares each size.

Brown (color #9):
two squares each size.

From the background fabric:
Cut forty-eight 4½" squares (11.4 cm), for large background squares.

Cut forty-eight 2½" squares (6.4 cm), for small background squares.

Cut six strips, 2" (5.1 cm) x WOF (width of fabric), for horizontal inner border. Vertical borders will be pieced.

Cut six strips, 3½" (8.9 cm) x WOF for outer border.

From contrasting border fabric:
Cut six strips, 2" (5.1 cm) x WOF.

From binding fabric:
Cut six strips, 2½" (6.4 cm) x WOF.

Dear Project Linus blanketeers,
I want to thank each of you for making blankets for Project Linus. When my boys Luke and Logan were born, Logan was in the NICU for five days. Five days may not seem long, but to a brand new mother they were forever, especially because Luke could not go into the NICU where Logan was. How thrilled I was when we were given two Project Linus blankets, one for each baby. We took Logan's to the hospital to keep in his bed, and Luke's was placed in the crib he and Logan would share as soon as Logan was well enough to come home.

The person who made and donated those blankets had no idea the inspiration she was following as she sewed and quilted those blankets. She didn't know when she chose the fabric for the front that it was the same fabric print that my baby blanket had been made from 25 years earlier. She didn't know as she made them the same on the front and different on the back that those blankets would go to twin boys who had a mother that wanted things to coordinate, not match. She also didn't know as she chose the white for the back of one and blue for the back of the other that those were the colors of the newborn hats each baby wore in the hospital—and the way we could tell who was who!

Assembly
Creating Block A

1 Place a small barbell square on the upper right corner of a large background square, right sides together. Draw a pencil line on the small square diagonally from corner to corner and stitch along the line.

2 Trim away the excess fabric ¼ inch (6 mm) from the stitched line and press the seam toward the barbell square (**Fig. 1**).

3 Repeat steps 1 and 2 to create 48 A blocks: two blocks from color #1, four blocks from color #2, six blocks from color #3, eight blocks from color #4, eight blocks from color #5, eight blocks from color #6, six blocks from color #7, four blocks from color #8, and two blocks from color #9.

Creating Block B

4 Stack a small background square on the upper right corner of a large barbell square, right sides together. In the same way as Block A, draw and stitch a diagonal line on the small square, trim the excess fabric, and press the seam (**Fig. 2**). Create 48 B blocks.

Creating the Barbell Blocks

5 Piece together a Block A and Block B as shown, using the same color blocks, to make the top half of the Barbell Block. Repeat to make the bottom half of the block (**Fig. 3**).

6 Piece together the top and bottom halves of the Barbell Block as shown (**Fig. 3**). Create 24 total Barbell Blocks.

Assembling the Quilt Top

7 Join the barbell blocks into six rows of four blocks each, as desired.

Adding Borders

8 Add borders as follows: Sew a horizontal inner border strip to the top and bottom edges of the quilt top. Then sew pieced vertical inner border strips to the side edges of the quilt.

(Continued from p. 33)

I know that each of you have been inspired to choose fabric, colors, and patterns that will be perfect for the child who will receive your blanket. These children may be in a situation like that of Luke and Logan. Perhaps they've had to stay in the hospital for a few days, or perhaps their brother or sister or mom or dad are in the hospital, and they are scared and need some comfort. How wonderful it is to see the smile that creeps across their faces as they realize they're getting a present: a soft cuddly blanket they can keep forever. Perhaps the child will be undergoing chemotherapy and will take the blanket with them to each of their visits. Perhaps the child's parent will be sent to serve our country for an extended period of time, and the blanket will be the hug that child needs. Or maybe the child will lose a family member and will cling to that blanket as Logan does to the one he received when Luke unexpectedly passed away two and a half years later. You never know the people you are touching because of your service—not just the child who receives the blanket, but also the parent or grandparent who can feel that for one instant or two, they can take the pain or fear or hurt away from their sweet child by wrapping them in that soft, beautiful blanket, the one YOU made for them. I know the Lord will bless you for your service, and as a parent, I thank you for that service.

Cari Balagna Shields

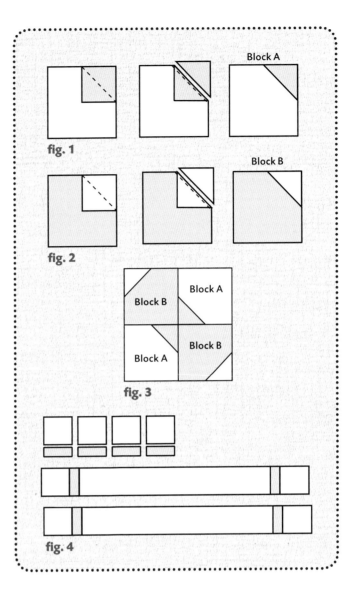

9 Measure the vertical sides of the quilt top. Sew together two 3½-inch (8.9 cm) x WOF outer border strips for each vertical side of the quilt. Trim these pieced outer vertical border strips to the measured size, saving and cutting the excess fabric to create four 3½-inch (8.9 cm) corner squares.

10 To the top and bottom edge of the quilt, add the horizontal contrasting border and horizontal outer border strips. Measure the vertical sides of the quilt, cut the pieced vertical contrasting border strips to size (save the remaining fabric), and sew these strips to the side edges of the quilt.

11 From the excess contrasting border strip fabric, cut four 2 x 3½-inch (5.1 x 8.9 cm) strips. Stitch them to one side of each of the four corner squares you cut in step 9 (**Fig. 4**).

12 Sew a corner square to each end of the vertical outer border strips from step 9 (**Fig. 4**). Then sew the strips to the side edges of the quilt.

Four years after Luke passed away, Cari designed this quilt pattern for Project Linus as a reflection of her experiences and struggles over the past four years. A simple four-patch block designed to represent exercise weights or barbells reminds us that we all have the strength and the power to overcome any adversity that we face. It is Cari's hope that when a child wraps this quilt around his or her shoulders, it will serve as a physical reminder that we do what we can when we are able and that there are always others by our side ready to help us lift our load.

Finishing the Quilt

13 Create the backing, following the instructions on page 15. Layer the backing, batting, and quilt top to make a quilt sandwich and baste the layers together.

14 Quilt as desired.

15 Sew the binding strips together and bind the edge of the quilt, following the Binding instructions, page 17.

Designed and pieced by Mary Balagna

Quilted by Linda Busbey

Covered in Love

These clever paper-pieced heart blocks have the lattice background built into the design. Just add the fabrics in order!

FINISHED QUILT SIZE
44" x 53" (111.8 x 134.6 cm)

FINISHED BLOCK SIZE
9" square (22.9 cm)

SEAM ALLOWANCE
¼" (6 mm)

MATERIALS
- Basic Supplies & Tools, page 11
- Foundation Heart Block Pattern, page 122
- **Heart background:** ½ yard (.5 m) of white tone-on-tone solid fabric (pieces #2, #3, #5, #6, #7)
- **Small heart section:** 20 scraps of light pink fabric, at least 2¼" x 3" (5.7 x 7.6 cm) (piece #1)
- **Large heart section:** 20 scraps of dark pink fabric, at least 3¼" x 4¾" (8.3 x 12 cm) (piece #4)
- **Lattice:** 1 yard (.9 m) of dark pink print fabric (pieces #12, #13, #14, #15)
- **Block corners:** ½ yard (.5 m) each of two light coordinating fabrics (pieces #16, #17, #18, and #19)
- **Heart block background, inner border:** 1⅓ yards (1.2 m) of fabric (pieces #8, #9, #10, #11)
- **Outer border:** 1½ yards (1.4 m) of fabric
- **Backing:** 2 yards (1.8 m) of backing fabric
- **Binding:** ½ yard (.5 m) of binding fabric

- **Batting:** 48" x 57" (121.9 x 144.8 cm)
- Paper for foundation piecing
- Glue stick

Note: If piecing vertical outer borders, 1 yard (.9 m) of fabric may be used.

Cutting
Pieces are cut slightly larger than necessary, to make sure that they adequately cover the assigned area for foundation piecing.

From heart background fabric (pieces #2, #3, #5, #6, #7):
Cut one strip, 3" (7.6 cm) x WOF (width of fabric), for piece #2.

Cut the piece #2 strip into 20 rectangles, 1¾" (4.4 cm) wide.

Cut two strips, 2½" (6.4 cm) x WOF, for pieces #3 and #5.

Cut the pieces #3 and #5 strips into twenty 2¼" (5.7 cm) squares.

Cut the squares diagonally from corner to corner—40 total triangles.

Cut two strips, 4" (10.2 cm) x WOF, for pieces #6 and #7.

Cut the pieces #6 and #7 strips into twenty 4" (10.2 cm) squares.

Cut the squares diagonally from corner to corner—40 total triangles.

From small heart section fabric (piece #1): Cut 20 rectangles, 2¼" x 3" (5.7 x 7.6 cm).

From large heart section fabric (piece #4): Cut 20 rectangles, 3¼" x 4¾" (8.3 x 12 cm).

From lattice fabric (pieces #12, #13, #14, and #15):
Cut four strips, 7½" (19 cm) x WOF.

Cut the strips into 80 rectangles, 1¾" x 7½" (4.4 x 19 cm).

From block corners fabric (pieces #16, #17, #18, and #19):
Cut two strips, 4½" (11.4 cm) x WOF, from each coordinating fabric.

Cut each set of strips into twenty 4½" (11.4 cm) squares—40 total block corner squares.

Cut the squares diagonally from corner to corner—80 total triangles.

From block background (pieces #8, #9, #10, and #11) and inner border fabric: Cut two strips, 1½" x 45½" (3.8 x 115.6 cm), for vertical (side) borders.

Cut two strips, 1½" x 38½" (3.8 x 97.8 cm), for horizontal (top and bottom) borders.

Cut forty 4½" (11.4 cm) squares, then cut in half diagonally.

From outer border fabric:
Cut two strips, 3½" x 47½" (8.9 x 120.7 cm), for vertical (side) borders.

Cut two strips, 3½" x 44½" (8.9 x 113 cm), for horizontal (top and bottom) borders.

From binding fabric:
Cut six strips, 2½" (6.4 cm) x WOF.

DIFFICULTY

A Stitch of Love

Service above self can be many different things. It could be saving a country from starvation, giving water to the homeless, or trying to stop pollution, but what about putting smiles on kids' faces? Isn't that supposed to be a main goal, especially on the faces of those in the hospital? They may have cancer or have had major surgery. Some kids have Cystic Fibrosis. Whatever the disease, kids need to smile.

I have Cystic Fibrosis, which affects my lungs and digestive system. I'm usually in the hospital once or twice each year, but unfortunately, this year it was three times, twice in two-and-a-half weeks. Over Spring Break, I was admitted to the hospital during the night because of a bad fever and horrible chills which could've been caused by an infection. My mom and I hadn't gotten a wink of sleep because residents kept coming in. As you can imagine, we were extremely tired!

Child Life employee, Tracey, came in with a beautiful pink ballerina blanket. As we unrolled it, my mom and I saw a poem. When I read it, I started crying, but they were good tears, tears of joy. I couldn't believe someone would do that for me. That blanket made my day.

I would love to be able to make some blankets to donate to the hospital to help other children in difficult situations. Many of my friends know how to make the blankets, so I'm going to start making plans for a party where we could make them. These blankets would mean a lot to kids and would make their day. If people would just see the look on kids' faces when they get something as special as a blanket, there would be a different perspective on what people do for kids and teens in need of help. Maybe giving blankets to children isn't saving a country. Sure, it's not stopping pollution, either. What it is, though, gives children a glimmer of hope of being out of the hospital, or at least making their room brighter than just white. Patients should smile, as Tracey made me, even if they are in the worst place to spend Spring Break!

Assembly
Creating the Blocks

1 Photocopy or trace the Foundation Heart Block Pattern onto the foundation paper. Make 20 copies, one for each heart block.

2 Paper piece each heart block in numerical order, following the Paper Piecing instructions on page 13.

Assembling the Quilt Top

3 Join the blocks into five rows of four blocks each.

Adding Borders

4 Add borders as follows: Sew a vertical inner border strip to each side edge of the quilt top. Then sew the remaining inner border strips to the top and bottom of the quilt. Add the outer border strips in the same way.

Finishing the Quilt

5 Create the backing, following the instructions on page 15. Layer the backing, batting, and quilt top to make a quilt sandwich and baste the layers together.

6 Quilt as desired.

7 Sew the binding strips together and bind the edge of the quilt, following the Binding instructions, page 17.

Handling It Together

Using kids' prints, fun tone-on-tone solids, and a simple white center, these signature blocks are the perfect way to offer group support and love to someone in need.

FINISHED QUILT SIZE
38" x 50" (96.5 x 127 cm)

FINISHED BLOCK SIZE
6½" square (16.5 cm)

SEAM ALLOWANCE
¼" (6 mm)

MATERIALS

- Basic Supplies & Tools, page 11
- Foundation Bar Block Pattern, page 123
- **Main bar fabric (for signing):** ½ yard (.5 m) of white or light fabric
- **Small triangle fabric:** ½ yard (.5 m) of one fabric or total from multiple fabrics
- **Large triangle fabric:** 1 yard (.9 m) of one fabric or total from multiple fabrics
- **Inner border:** ¼ yard (.2 m) of fabric
- **Outer border:** ¾ yard (.7 m) of fabric
- **Backing:** 2 yards (1.8 m) of backing fabric
- **Binding:** ½ yard (.5 m) of binding fabric
- **Batting:** 44" x 53" (109.2 x 134.6 cm)
- Paper for foundation piecing
- Glue stick
- Fabric markers or paints

Note: For identical blocks, use the same fabric for all the small and large triangles. For a scrappier look, use whatever fabric scraps you've got on hand.

Cutting

Pieces are cut slightly larger than necessary to make sure that they adequately cover the assigned area for foundation piecing.

From the white bar fabric (piece #1):
Cut five strips, 3½" (8.9 cm) x WOF (width of fabric).

Cut those strips into thirty-five 6" x 3½" (15.2 x 8.9 cm) rectangles.

From the small triangle fabric (pieces #2 and #3):
Cut four strips, 3½" (8.9 cm) x WOF.

Cut those strips into thirty-five 3½" (8.9 cm) squares. If you're using scraps, cut all your scraps to 3½" (8.9 cm) squares.

Cut all squares in half on the diagonal.

From the large triangle fabric (pieces #4 and #5):
Cut five strips, 5½" (14 cm) x WOF.

Cut those strips into thirty-five 5½" (14 cm) squares. If you're using scraps, cut all your scraps to 5½" (14 cm) squares.

Cut all squares in half on the diagonal.

From inner border fabric:
Cut six strips, 1½" (3.8 cm) x WOF.

From outer border fabric:
Cut six strips, 3½" (8.9 cm) x WOF.

From binding fabric:
Cut six strips, 2½" (6.4 cm) x WOF.

DIFFICULTY

Designed and pieced by Mary Balagna

Quilted by Linda Kirby

Assembly
Creating the Blocks

1 Photocopy or trace the Foundation Bar Block Pattern onto the foundation paper. Make 35 copies, one for each bar block.

2 Paper piece the bar block in numerical order, following the Paper Piecing instructions on page 13.

3 It is easier to sign and embellish the blocks before you assemble the quilt top. Stabilize the back of the bar fabric, embellish with fabric markers or paint, and set the fabric following the manufacturer's directions.

Assembling the Quilt Top

4 Join the blocks into seven rows of five blocks each.

Dear Project Linus,

I am the aunt of three very happy children that received quilts from your organization yesterday. They were given quilts that had squares made by each of their classmates after they were in an accident that killed their mother and their two-year-old brother. They have had a lot of support, but I have to say that I am very thankful for your organization. My nephew has been asking for a quilt for two or three years. His sister, Sierra, was given one for Christmas from her grandmother on her dad's side, and since then he has been asking for one for himself. He is now paralyzed from the accident and has to be in a wheelchair for the rest of his life. He is eight years old. These are some of the bravest children I know, and I love them very much.

Again I say thank you for all you have done to make these children happy. It is enough for me to know they have something to be happy about.

Adding Borders

5 Add borders as follows: Sew a vertical inner border strip to each side of the quilt top. Then sew the remaining inner border strips to the top and bottom of the quilt. Add the outer border strips in the same way.

Finishing the Quilt

6 Create the backing, following the instructions on page 15. Layer the backing, batting, and quilt top to make a quilt sandwich and baste the layers together.

7 Quilt as desired.

8 Sew the binding strips together and bind the edge of the quilt, following the Binding instructions, page 17.

Designed by Debbi Dillman and Mary Balagna

Pieced and quilted by Mary Balagna

Pretty Pockets

A novelty fabric, a coordinating fabric, and a border fabric create the perfect background for a group of pretty—and handy!—pockets.

FINISHED QUILT SIZE
45" x 57" (114.3 x 144.8 cm)

FINISHED BLOCK SIZE
6" square (15.2 cm)

FINISHED POCKET WITH FLAP
5¾" x 6" (14.6 x 15.2 cm)

SEAM ALLOWANCE
¼" (6 mm)

MATERIALS
- Basic Supplies & Tools, page 11
- Pocket Template, page 118
- **Novelty squares:** 1¼ yards (1.1 m) of novelty print fabric A
- **Coordinating squares:** 1¼ yards (1.1 m) of fabric B
- **Pockets, flaps/lining:** 18 fabric scraps, each at least 6½" x 9½" (16.5 x 24.1 cm)
- **Inner border and binding:** 1¼ yards (1.1 m) of fabric
- **Backing:** 1¾ yards (1.6 m) of backing fabric
- **Batting**: 49" x 61" (124.5 x 154.9 cm), plus nine batting scraps for pockets, each at least 6½ x 9½" (16.5 x 24.1 cm)
- **Pocket embellishments:** 2¾ yards (2.5 m) of lace and nine appliqué flowers

Cutting

From novelty squares fabric A:
Cut six strips, each 6½" (16.5 cm) x WOF (width of fabric).

Cut strips into 6½" (16.5 cm) squares—32 total squares.

From coordinating squares fabric B:
Cut six strips, each 6½" (16.5 cm) x WOF.

Cut strips into 6½" (16.5 cm) squares—32 total squares.

From pocket fabric, pocket flaps/ lining fabric, and batting scraps:
Cut nine rectangles from each set of fabrics and batting, 6½" x 9½" (16.5 x 24.1 cm).

Photocopy or trace the Pocket Template on page 118. Using the template, cut nine ovals from each rectangle.

From inner border fabric:
Cut six strips for inner borders, 2" (5.1 cm) x WOF.

Cut four rectangles from one inner border strip, each 2" x 6½" (5.1 x 16.5 cm).

Cut six strips for binding, 2½" (6.4 cm) x WOF.

DIFFICULTY

Dear Project Linus,
My cousin received one of the blankets made by Project Linus. I wanted to thank you for being a part of such an organization and for offering your services to her. She lost her battle with cancer on New Year's Eve. During that time, we were told that she carried the Project Linus blanket with her to every doctor appointment she had and slept with it every night. It obviously meant a lot to her.

Assembly
Creating the Pockets

1 Layer one pocket oval and one pocket flap/lining oval, right sides together, on top of one batting oval. Stitch around the oval using a walking foot, leaving an opening approximately 1½ inches (3.8 cm) for turning (**Fig. 1**).

2 Clip the curves, turn, and hand stitch the opening closed. Press.

3 Add embellishments (lace, appliqué, etc.) around the flap edge of the oval. (**Fig. 2**)

4 Repeat steps 1–3 to create nine pockets.

Assembling the Quilt Top

5 Piece together novelty and coordinating fabric squares as shown (**Fig. 3**). You will need the following strip sets for each row:
- Four of Strip Set A.
- Five of Strip Set B.

6 Join together Strip Sets A and three of Strip Sets B to make the center section of the quilt top, alternating sets as shown in the sample photograph.

*How can I help?
Make a blanket and take it to your local chapter.
They will make sure it gets into the arms of a child in need.*

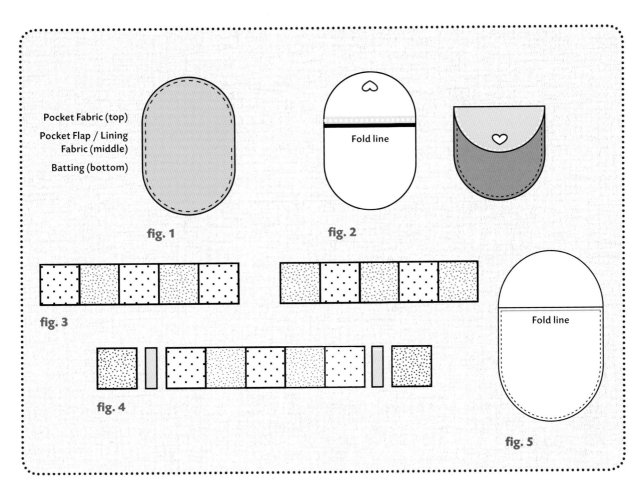

Pocket Fabric (top)
Pocket Flap / Lining Fabric (middle)
Batting (bottom)

fig. 1

Fold line

fig. 2

fig. 3

fig. 4

Fold line

fig. 5

Adding Borders

7 Add inner borders as follows: Sew an inner border strip to each side edge of the quilt top. Press seams toward the inner borders.

8 Piece together three novelty and four coordinating fabric squares in the same way as the strip sets. Repeat to make a second column of squares. Join a column to each vertical inner border strip.

9 Piece together two horizontal inner border strips, 2 x 45½ inches (5.1 x 115.6 cm). Join a pieced strip to each horizontal side of the quilt top.

10 Sew a novelty square and an inner border rectangle to the end of each strip set left over from step 6 (**Fig. 4**). Sew these pieced rows to the top and bottom of the quilt top.

11 Pin and sew the pockets onto the quilt top as desired, stitching around each pocket from one side of the fold line to the opposite side of the fold line. Backstitch at the fold line on both sides to secure (**Fig. 5**).

12 Fold down the pocket flaps and tack in place.

Finishing the Quilt

13 Create the backing, following the instructions on page 15. Layer the backing, batting, and quilt top to make a quilt sandwich and baste the layers together.

14 Quilt as desired.

15 Sew the binding strips together and bind the edge of the quilt, following the Binding instructions, page 17.

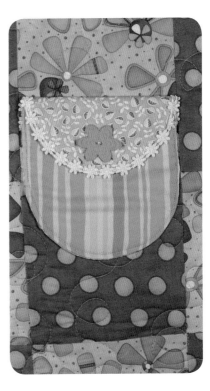

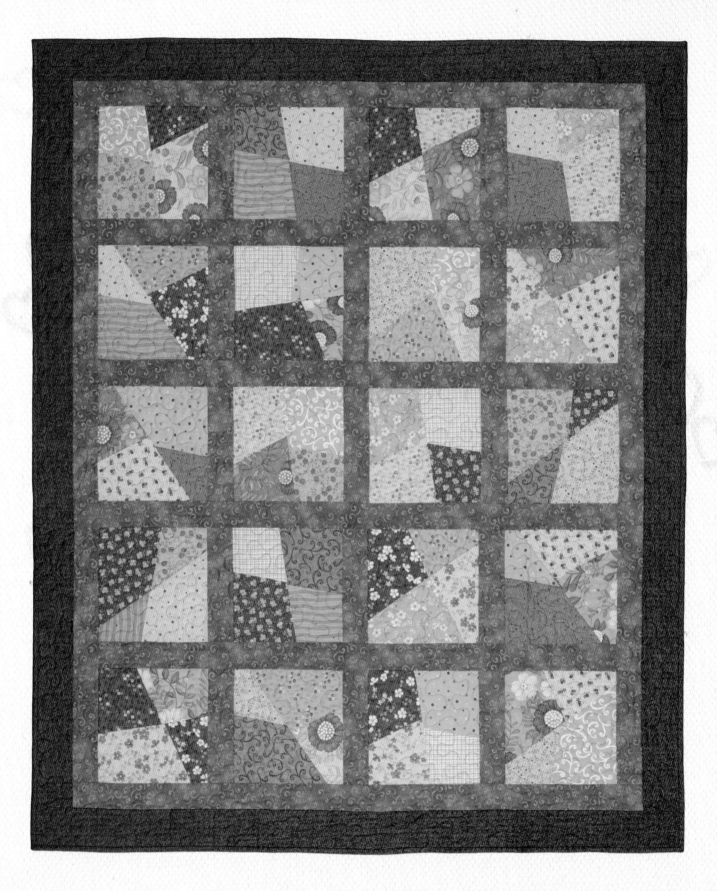

Designed by Patricia Hickey   Pieced by Mary Balagna
Quilted by Linda Kirby

Crazy 4 You

Stack, cut, and sew squares together again to create this crazy quilt design—the perfect handmade hug.

FINISHED QUILT SIZE
50" x 60½" (127 x 153.7 cm)

FINISHED BLOCK SIZE
8½" square (21.6 cm)
(size approximate)

SEAM ALLOWANCE
¼" (6 mm)

MATERIALS
- Basic Supplies & Tools, page 11
- **Blocks:** 20 scraps of assorted fabrics, each at least 10" square (25.4 cm)
- **Sashing, inner border:** 1 yard (.9 m) of contrasting fabric
- **Outer border, binding:** 1⅓ yards (1.2 m) of coordinating fabric
- **Backing:** 3 yards (2.7 m) of backing fabric
- **Batting:** 54" x 65" (137.2 x 165.1 cm)

Note: Assorted collections of precut 10" (25.4 cm) fabric squares make finding the right amount of fabric for this project quick and easy.

Cutting
From assorted fabric squares:
Cut twenty 10" (25.4 cm) squares.

From sashing, inner border fabric:
Cut 13 strips, 2½" (6.4 cm) x WOF (width of fabric). Set aside five strips for the inner border.

Cut four of the strips into four units each, approximately 11" (27.9 cm) long, for vertical sashing between blocks.

Note: The length of these four units will be determined by the unfinished block size after "squaring up" the blocks. For example, if the unfinished block size after "squaring up" is 9" (22.9 cm), then cut the 15 sashing strips to 9" (22.9 cm).

From outer border, binding fabric:
Cut eight strips, 3½" (8.9 cm) x WOF, for outer border.

Cut six strips, 2½" (6.4 cm) x WOF, for binding.

DIFFICULTY

Assembly
Creating the Blocks

1 Neatly stack the assorted fabric squares edge to edge, 10 squares per stack. Angle your ruler vertically on the first fabric stack and randomly cut through the stack of fabric, using a sharp rotary cutting blade. Repeat with the second stack of fabric (**Fig. 1**).

2 Move the left piece from the top of each stack to the bottom. Two different fabrics are now on top. Sew each pair together, creating 20 new two-patch blocks. Do not sew pieces of the same fabric together in any one block (**Fig. 2**). Press the seams to one side and neatly stack the squares again, making two stacks of 10 pieced two-patch blocks.

3 Angle your ruler on the first fabric stack, and cut through the stack at a random angle, cutting across the first sewn seam. Repeat with the second stack (**Fig. 3**).

4 Move the right piece from the top of each stack to the bottom and sew each pair together, creating 20 four-patch "crazy" blocks. Press the seams in one direction (**Fig. 3**).

5 The blocks will be slightly uneven. Trim the smallest block and measure it to determine the size to which to cut the remaining blocks, approximately 9 inches square (22.9 cm). Trim the 20 blocks to size.

How can I make a monetary donation? Go to www.projectlinus.org/ donations.

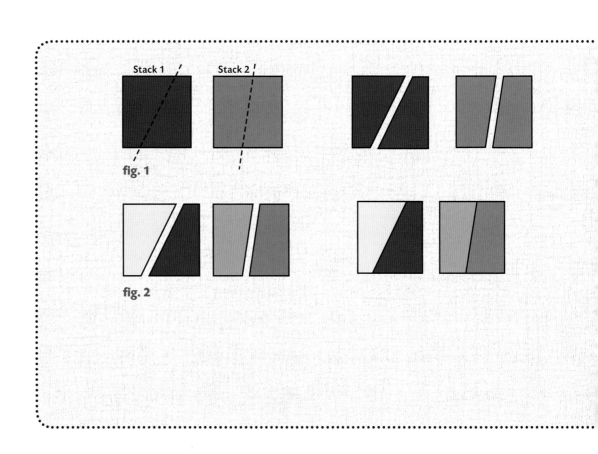

Stack 1 Stack 2

fig. 1

fig. 2

Assembling the Quilt Top

6 Adjust the length of the short sashing strips to the length of your blocks. Join together the blocks and the short strips in five rows of four blocks each, as shown **(Fig. 4)**. Join together the horizontal rows with the long sashing strips.

Note: Always measure the size of the blocks and adjust the length of sashing strips accordingly, as needed.

Adding Borders

7 Add borders as follows: Sew an inner border strip to the top and bottom edges of the quilt top. Then sew the remaining inner border strips the to side edges of the quilt.

8 Sew the outer border strips to the top and bottom edges of the quilt top. Then sew the remaining outer border strips to the side edges of the quilt.

Finishing the Quilt

9 Create the backing, following the instructions on page 15. Layer the backing, batting, and quilt top to make a quilt sandwich and baste the layers together.

10 Quilt as desired.

11 Sew the binding strips together and bind the edge of the quilt, following the Binding instructions, page 17.

fig. 3

fig. 4

Designed and pieced by Cheryl Hughes

Quilted by Ron and Kay Gerard

E-I-E-I-O

Inspired by Old McDonald's tune, pieced blocks and a little bit of appliqué will help you create this colorful barnyard.

FINISHED QUILT SIZE
50" x 60" (127 x 152.4 cm)

SEAM ALLOWANCE
¼" (6 mm)

MATERIALS
- Basic Supplies & Tools, page 11
- Animal Templates, page 124
- **Animal appliqués:** 12 fabric scraps, each at least 10" square (25.4 cm)
- **Barn:** ¼ yard (.2 m) each of 4 red fabrics
- **Barn windows, doors:** 4 fabric scraps, each at least 4½" x 10" (11.4 cm x 25.4 cm)
- **Fence, letters:** 1¼ yards (1.1 m) of dark brown fabric
- **Background fabric:** 2¾ yards (2.5 m) of neutral fabric
- **Backing:** 3 yards (2.7 m) of backing fabric
- **Binding:** ½ yard (.5 m) of binding fabric
- **Batting:** 54" x 64" (137.2 x 162.6 cm)
- 1½ yards (1.4 m) of paper-backed fusible web
- **Optional:** Embroidery needle and floss

DIFFICULTY

Cutting

From appliqué fabrics:
Photocopy the templates on page 124. Using the templates, cut out each farm animal twice—12 total animal appliqués.

From each barn fabric:
Cut two rectangles, 3½" x 5½" (8.9 x 14 cm).

Cut two rectangles, 1½" x 4½" (3.8 x 11.4 cm).

Cut one rectangle, 1½" x 10½" (3.8 x 26.7 cm).

Cut two rectangles, 2½" x 4½" (6.4 x 11.4 cm).

From barn windows, doors fabrics:
Cut one rectangle, 4½" x 3½" (11.4 x 8.9 cm), from each fabric— 4 total barn windows.

Cut one rectangle, 4½" x 6½" (11.4 x 16.5 cm), from each fabric— 4 total barn doors.

From fence, letters fabric:
Cut 18 strips, 1½" (3.8 cm) x WOF (width of fabric), for fence rails.

Cut four of the strips into rectangles, 5½" (14 cm) long, for fence posts— 22 total posts.

Cut four strips, 2½" (6.4 cm) x WOF, for letters.

From the letter strips, cut and label the following:
Label A: Cut six rectangles, 2½" x 7½" (6.4 x 19 cm).

Label B: Cut four rectangles, 2½" x 6½" (6.4 x 16.5 cm).

Label C: Cut sixteen 2½" (6.4 cm) squares.

Label D: Cut two rectangles, 2½" x 5½" (6.4 x 14 cm).

From background fabric:
Cut eight 3½" (8.9 cm) squares for barns.

Cut 21 strips, 1½" (3.8 cm) x WOF, for fence borders.

Cut twelve 10½" (26.7 cm) squares for the animal block backgrounds.

Cut three strips, 2½" (6.4 cm) x WOF, for letters.

For the letter background strips, cut and label the following:
Label E: Cut ten 2½" (6.4 cm) squares.

Label F: Cut two rectangles, 2½" x 1½" (6.4 x 3.8 cm).

Label G: Cut four rectangles, 2½" x 9½" (6.4 x 24.1 cm).

Label H: Cut two rectangles, 2½" x 6½" (6.4 x 16.5 cm).

Label I: Cut six rectangles, 2½" x 3½" (6.4 x 8.9 cm).

Label J: Cut three rectangles, 2½" x 4½" (6.4 x 11.4 cm).

From binding fabric:
Cut six strips, 2½" (6.4 cm) x WOF.

Assembly

Creating the Animal Blocks

1 Appliqué an animal shape to the center of each 10½-inch (26.7 cm) background square, using the fusible web and following the Appliqué instructions, page 12. Add embroidery or other embellishments if desired.

Creating the Barn Blocks

2 Draw a pencil line diagonally from corner to corner on the wrong side of two 3½-inch (8.9 cm) background squares. Stack each marked square on a 3½ x 5½-inch (8.9 x 14 cm) barn rectangle, as shown, right sides together, and stitch along the marked lines (**Fig. 1**).

3 Draw a diagonal line ¼ inch (6 mm) from your stitching and trim along the line to make the seam allowance for each. Discard the corner pieces. Press the seams toward the barn fabric.

4 Make two corner pieces; the second will be the reverse image of the first. Label the first piece "Corner" and the second "Corner Reversed." (**Fig. 2**)

5 Piece together two 1½ x 4½-inch (3.8 x 11.4 cm) barn rectangles and a barn window piece as shown. Join the Corner and Corner Reversed pieces to each side of the barn window section, creating the top of the block (**Fig. 3**).

6 Piece together two 2½ x 4½-inch (6.4 x 11.4 cm) barn rectangles and a barn door piece, creating the bottom of the block.

7 Piece together the top of the block, a 1½ x 10½-inch (3.8 x 26.7 cm) barn rectangle, and the bottom of the block as shown (**Fig. 4**).

8 Sew a line down the middle of the door using a tight satin stitch, creating a double barn door.

9 Repeat steps 2–8 to create four total Barn Blocks.

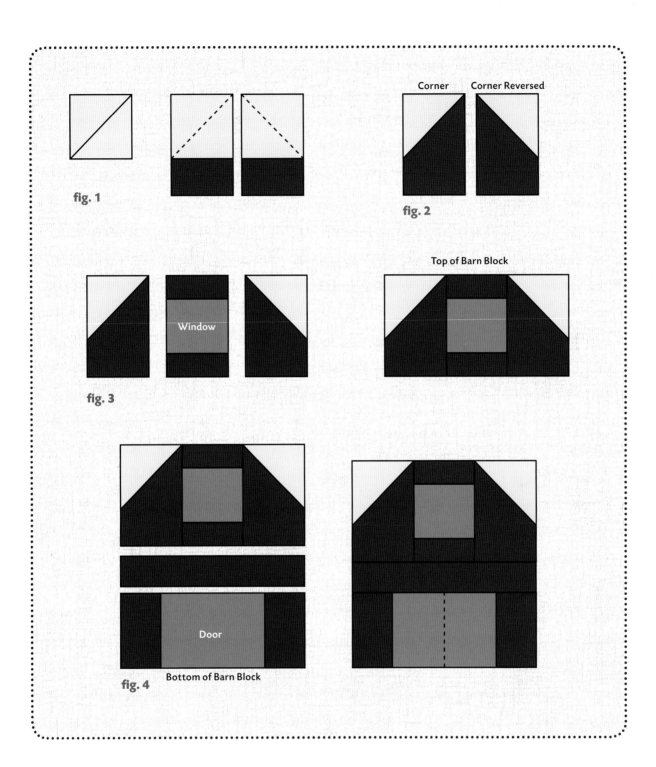

fig. 1

Corner　　Corner Reversed

fig. 2

Window

fig. 3

Top of Barn Block

Door

fig. 4　Bottom of Barn Block

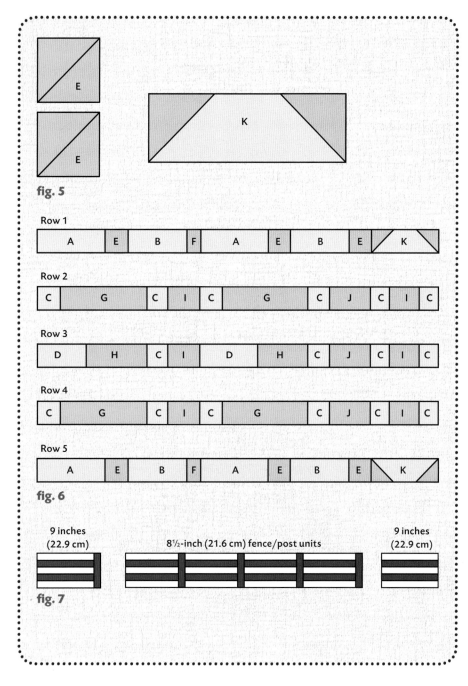

fig. 5

Row 1

| A | E | B | F | A | E | B | E | K |

Row 2

| C | G | C | I | C | G | C | J | C | I | C |

Row 3

| D | H | C | I | D | H | C | J | C | I | C |

Row 4

| C | G | C | I | C | G | C | J | C | I | C |

Row 5

| A | E | B | F | A | E | B | E | K |

fig. 6

9 inches (22.9 cm)   8½-inch (21.6 cm) fence/post units   9 inches (22.9 cm)

fig. 7

Creating the Letter Blocks

10 Draw a diagonal pencil line from corner to corner on the wrong side of two background E squares. Stack one marked square on each end of a letter A rectangle as shown, right sides together, and stitch along the marked line (**Fig. 5**).

11 Draw a diagonal line ¼ inch (6 mm) from your stitching as shown and trim along the line to make the seam allowance. Discard the corner pieces and press the seam allowances toward the letter fabric.

12 Repeat steps 9 and 10 to make a second piece and label both pieces "K."

13 Piece together the labeled letter pieces in the following order as follows, pressing each row in opposite directions (**Fig. 6**):

Row 1: A, E, B, F, A, E, B, E, K.

Row 2: C, G, C, I, C, G, C, J, C, I, C.

Row 3: D, H, C, I, D, H, C, J, C, I, C.

Row 4: C, G, C, I, C, G, C, J, C, I, C.

Row 5: A, E, B, F, A, E, B, E, K.

14 Join the rows together to create the large E-I-E-I-O block.

Assembling the Quilt Top

15 Join the barn and animal blocks together in rows, using the sample photograph as a guide. Then join the rows.

Adding Borders

16 Piece together a fence strip set by alternating three background fence border strips with two fence rail strips. Repeat to create seven total strip sets.

17 Cut the fence strip sets into eighteen 8½-inch (21.6 cm) units and eight 9-inch (22.9 cm) units.

18 Join a fence post to one end of each 8½-inch (21.6 cm) units and to one end of four of the 9-inch (22.9 cm) units **(Fig. 7)**.

19 Join together four 8½-inch (21.6 cm) fence/post units, one 9-inch (22.9 cm) fence/post unit, and one single 9-inch (22.9 cm). Repeat to create a total of two horizontal border strips.

20 Join together five 8½-inch (21.6 cm) fence/post units, one 9-inch (22.9 cm) fence/post unit, and one single 9-inch (22.9 cm) unit in the same way. Repeat to create a total of two vertical border strips.

21 Add borders to the quilt top, following the Adding a Border with a Mitered Corners instructions, page 15.

Finishing the Quilt

22 Create the backing, following the instructions on page 15. Layer the backing, batting, and quilt top to make a quilt sandwich and baste the layers together.

23 Quilt as desired.

24 Sew the binding strips together and bind the edge of the quilt, following the Binding instructions, page 17.

Designed and pieced by Mary Balagna

Quilted by Althea Warner

Handmade With Love

Combining 3-D pinwheels with a star block pattern brings this quilt to life with dimensional fun. This quilt is dedicated to our founder, Karen Loucks Rinedollar.

FINISHED QUILT SIZE
44" x 56" (111.8 x 142.2 cm)

FINISHED BLOCK SIZE
12" square (30.5 cm)

SEAM ALLOWANCE
¼" (6 mm)

MATERIALS
- Basic Supplies & Tools, page 11
- **Star block fabric #1:** 1 yard (.9 m) of yellow fabric
- **Star block fabric #2:** 1 yard (.9 m) of green fabric
- **Pinwheel background fabric:** ½ yard (.5 m) of light blue fabric
- **Pinwheels:** 12 scraps of assorted fabric, each at least 3½" x 14" (8.9 x 35.6 cm)
- **Inner border:** ⅓ yard (.3 m) of fabric
- **Outer border:** 1½ yards (1.4 m) of fabric
- **Backing:** 1¾ yards (1.6 m) of backing fabric
- **Binding:** ½ yard (.5 m) of binding fabric
- **Batting:** 48" x 60" (121.9 x 152.4 cm)

DIFFICULTY

Cutting

From yellow star block fabric #1:
Cut 10 strips, 3½" (8.9 cm) x WOF (width of fabric).

Cut six of the strips into seventy-two 3½" (8.9 cm) squares.

Cut the remaining four strips into 24 rectangles, 3½" x 6½" (8.9 x 16.5 cm).

From green star block fabric #2:
Cut 10 strips, 3½" (8.9 cm) x WOF.

Cut six of the strips into seventy-two 3½" (8.9 cm) squares.

Cut the remaining four strips into 24 rectangles, 3½" x 6½" (8.9 x 16.5 cm).

From light blue fabric:
Cut four strips, 3½" (8.9 cm) x WOF.

Cut the strips into forty-eight 3½" (8.9 cm) squares.

From assorted pinwheel fabrics:
Cut four 3½" (8.9 cm) squares from each fabric—48 total squares.

From inner border fabric:
Cut five strips, 1½" (3.8 cm) x WOF.

Cut four 3½" (8.9 cm) squares (for the corner squares).

From outer border fabric:
Cut four strips, 3½" (8.9 cm) x WOF.

From binding fabric:
Cut six strips, 2½" (6.4 cm) x WOF.

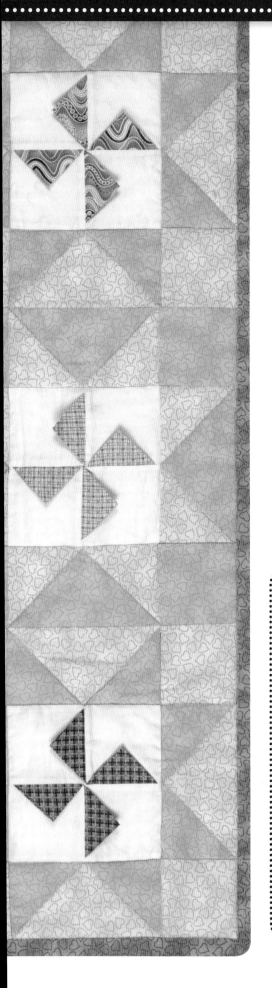

Assembly
Creating Block A

You will need four pinwheel squares, four light blue fabric squares, eight yellow squares, four green squares, and four green rectangles to create each block.

1 Fold four pinwheel fabric squares in half diagonally, matching points. Press. Fold in half again, matching points. Press **(Fig. 1)**.

2 Pin the raw edge of each folded pinwheel blade to one side of a light blue square and baste in place, ⅛ inch (3 mm) from the edge of each square **(Fig. 2)**. Repeat this four times.

3 Sew together two squares, right sides together, to form the top half of the pinwheel shape, and then sew together the remaining two squares to form the bottom half, as shown.

Press the seams toward the light blue fabric. Join the top row to the bottom row, creating the pinwheel center of the block. Press the seam in one direction **(Fig. 3)**. Repeat to create six pinwheel blocks.

4 Draw a pencil line diagonally from corner to corner on the wrong side of eight yellow squares.

5 Place two marked yellow squares on one green rectangle, end-to-end and right sides together, covering the surface area of the rectangle. The marked lines should meet to form a triangle shape. Stitch along the marked lines and cut away the excess fabric ¼ inch (6 mm) from your stitching to form one flying geese block. Press the seams toward the triangles **(Fig. 4)**. Repeat to create four total flying geese blocks.

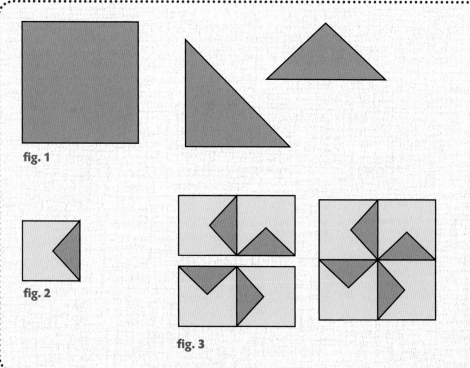

fig. 1

fig. 2

fig. 3

6 Sew two flying geese blocks to the opposite sides of the pinwheel center of the block. Press the seams toward the pinwheel center (**Fig. 5**).

7 Sew a green square to each end of the two remaining flying geese blocks. Press the seams toward the corner squares. Then sew these strips to the remaining sides of the block and press the seams toward the flying geese blocks (**Fig. 5**).

8 Repeat steps 1–7 to create six total A blocks.

Creating Block B

You will need four pinwheel squares, four light blue fabric squares, eight green squares, four yellow squares, and four yellow rectangles to create each block.

9 Follow the instructions for creating Block A, substituting the green fabric as the "star" fabric and the yellow fabric as the "background" fabric. When pressing the blocks, press the seams in the opposite directions as Block A so that the seams abut when joining the blocks. Create six total B blocks.

Assembling the Quilt Top

10 Join the blocks into four rows of three blocks each, alternating blocks A and B. Press the seams toward the B blocks.

Adding the Borders

11 Add inner borders as follows: Sew an inner border strip to each side of the quilt top. Then sew the remaining inner border strips to the top and bottom edges of the quilt.

12 Add outer borders following the Adding a Border with Corner Squares instructions, page 14: Sew the outer border strips to the side edges of the quilt top, centering the strips along the edges. Sew a corner square to each end of the remaining outer border strips and sew the long strips to the top and bottom edges.

Finishing the Quilt

13 Create the backing, following the instructions on page 15. Layer the backing, batting, and quilt top to make a quilt sandwich and baste the layers together.

14 Quilt as desired.

15 Sew the binding strips together and bind the edge of the quilt, following the Binding instructions, page 17.

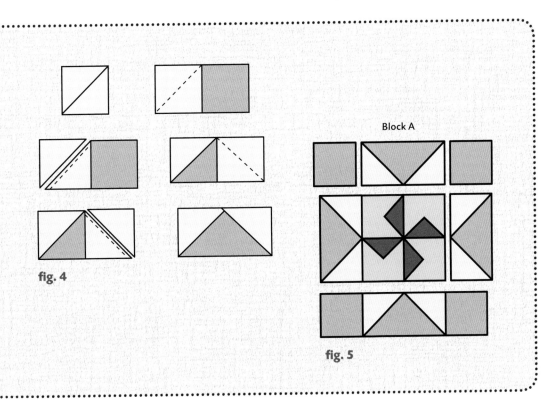

fig. 4

Block A

fig. 5

Designed and pieced by Carol Babbitt

Quilted by Mary Balagna

Remember Who You Are

Inspired by and dedicated to Carol's mom, Opal Larsen, this quilt is a cheerful reminder of a child's worth and a mother's love.

FINISHED QUILT SIZE
56" x 63" (142.2 x 160 cm)

FINISHED BLOCK SIZE
8" square (20.3 cm)

SEAM ALLOWANCE
¼" (6 mm)

MATERIALS
- Basic Supplies & Tools, page 11
- Templates, page 125
- **Background:** 1½ yards (1.4 m) total of two background fabrics
- **Sashing:** 1½ yards (1.4 m) of fabric
- **Inner border:** 1¾ yards (1.6 m)
- **Outer Border:** 1 yard (.9 m)
- **Children:** 12 assorted tone-on-tone fabric scraps, each at least 6" x 7" (15.2 x 17.8 cm)
- **Hair:** 12 assorted tone-on-tone fabric scraps
- **Clothing:** 18 assorted fabric scraps
- **Hearts:** 13 assorted fabric scraps, each at least 7" square (17.8 cm)
- **Backing:** 3½ yards (3.2 m)
- **Binding:** ¾ yard (.7 m)
- **Batting:** 62" x 67" (157.5 x 170.2 cm)
- 3 yards (2.7 m) of paper-backed fusible web

Cutting

From background fabrics:
Cut six strips total, 8½" (21.6 cm) x WOF (width of fabric).

Cut the strips into twenty-five 8½" (21.6 cm) squares total, 12 in one color and 13 in the other.

From sashing fabric:
Cut one strip, 8½" (21.6 cm) x WOF.

Cut the strip into 20 units, 2" x 8½" (5.1 x 21.6 cm), for vertical sashing strips.

Cut four strips, 4½" (11.4 cm) x measured length of row (about 44" [111.8 cm]), before inner and outer borders are added.

From inner border fabric:
Cut and piece two strips that measure 2" x 45" (5.1 x 114.3 cm) (horizontal) and two that measure 2" x 55" (5.1 x 139.7 cm) (vertical) (size approximate).

From outer border fabric:
Cut and piece two strips that measure 4" x 51" (10.2 x 129.5 cm) (horizontal) and two that measure 4" x 63" (10.2 x 160 cm) (vertical) (size approximate).

From binding fabric:
Cut seven 2½" (6.4 cm) wide x WOF strips.

DIFFICULTY

My mother taught me many things as a young girl that would bring me happiness in my life. She seemed to know the words to every nursery rhyme ever written or told. She constantly recited silly poems and nearly always woke me up with "Good Morning, Merry Sunshine," much to my chagrin at the time. And like many other children, my own included, I never left the house without hearing "Remember Who You Are." I knew I was loved, that I was special, and that I was always in her heart. She set me on a path that would bring me great joy and satisfaction later in my life, and neither of us was aware of how much that would mean to me. Because of her, I had an opportunity as a six year old to help take a fruit basket to an elderly woman in our neighborhood. I remember the sweet woman, I remember her home, and I remember the bright sunny day. I've never forgotten the enormous feeling of gratification that came from helping someone else. I've chased that feeling most of my life, many times catching it.

For many years I was a stay-at-home mom, very busy with two active boys. When my youngest started first grade in 1998, I knew the timing was right to really pursue my ambitions to become active in volunteering. But what to do?

(Continued on p. 62)

(Continued from p. 61)

I wanted something that utilized my talents and interests and of course, served others. I began to do some charity sewing projects here and there and had a great time. Then, one day I saw an article in our local paper about a new organization called Project Linus. It was a perfect fit for me, and I was anxious to get started. I contacted the local chapter coordinator and made an appointment to visit with her. Soon I was working towards a personal goal of making 100 blankets for the local chapter. For reasons that will become apparent, that never happened. I had never done any "real" quilting at that time. I had never pieced a top and honestly couldn't see the point in cutting up perfectly good fabric just to sew it back together. My blankets were generally whole cloth blankets: two layers of whole fabric with

batting in between. We stretched them on quilt frames and tied them with yarn or perle cotton. A simple rolled edge provided the binding. I loved those quilts and still do today.

Before long, the chapter coordinator decided that she needed to step down so that she could return to school. She asked me to take over as chapter coordinator, and I was excited to do so. At first, I was very overwhelmed by the prospect of stepping out of my comfort zone. I had never done anything like that before. What I found is that I was able to do many things I didn't think I could do. That is a lesson I continue to learn each and every day. I had no idea what lay ahead of me.

I led the activities of the Northern Utah chapter for two years and had a great time and a lot of success. We delivered

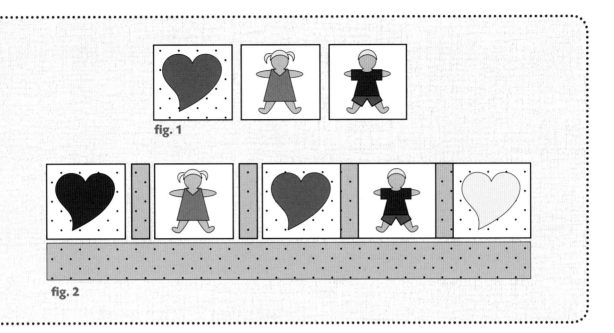

fig. 1

fig. 2

Assembly

Creating the Blocks

1 Photocopy or trace the templates on page 125. Using the templates, cut out the body shapes, hair, clothing, and hearts from the assorted fabric scraps—assemble 12 total boys and girls and 13 hearts.

2 Appliqué each assembled shape to the center of an 8½-inch (21.6 cm) background square, using the fusible web and following the Appliqué instructions, page 12 **(Fig. 1)**.

Assembling the Quilt Top

3 Join together the blocks with the vertical sashing strips as shown, alternating heart, boy, and girl blocks, to create five rows of five blocks each **(Fig. 2)**.

4 Measure the length of each of the five rows of blocks and take an average of their length. Cut the four horizontal 2-inch (5.1 cm) sashing strips to the measured average length and join the horizontal rows together with these strips. Press the seams toward the vertical sashing. **(Fig. 2)**

Note: Always measure the size of the finished blocks and adjust the length of the sashing strips accordingly, as needed.

blankets to children in several area hospitals and social service agencies. Later when my husband took a job in the Midwest, we moved to Minnesota for a short time, and I also coordinated a chapter there. I loved my volunteer work with Project Linus. I knew these blankets helped children, and I knew that the work brought satisfaction to our volunteers.

In June of 2000, I attended the 2nd annual Project Linus Conference in Denver, Colorado. Conference was, and is, a great opportunity for chapter coordinators to come together for education and inspiration. My husband, who has always been my biggest supporter, attended with me. At the end of one day we were going back upstairs to our room and found ourselves on the elevator with another attendee, Mary Balagna, and her daughter.

We said hello, traded small talk, and found we had several things in common besides Project Linus. I immediately liked Mary, and I felt like I had made a new friend. Again, I had no idea what the future held, or how true those words would prove.

I had also made some good friends of members of the Project Linus board of directors. They are a wonderful group of women who spent countless hours forming the foundation of this organization. Karen Loucks, Betsy Elliott, Laurie Huffman, and others were very committed to Project Linus. However, my friends shared with me that there were some concerns about the future of the organization. It was a very difficult time and my heart went out to them. While the organization was solvent and in good standing, the board and officers no longer agreed on the direction it

(Continued on p. 65)

Adding Borders

5 Add borders as follows: Sew an inner border strip to each side of the quilt top. Then sew the remaining inner border strips to the top and bottom edges of the quilt.

6 Sew the outer border strips to the top and bottom edges of the quilt top. Then sew the remaining outer border strips to the side edges.

Finishing the Quilt

7 Create the backing, following the instructions on page 15. Layer the backing, batting, and quilt top to make a quilt sandwich and baste the layers together.

8 Quilt as desired.

9 Sew the binding strips together and bind the edge of the quilt, following the Binding instructions, page 17.

Project Linus welcomes blankets of all styles, including quilts, tied comforters, fleece blankets, crocheted or knitted afghans, and receiving blankets in child-friendly colors.

(Continued from p. 63)

should take. They told me that in all likelihood they would disband Project Linus by the end of the year. I couldn't imagine my life without Project Linus. I had finally found the perfect volunteer work. I loved every minute spent on my coordinator duties and in making blankets for children. My final comments to them were to please give someone else the opportunity to lead Project Linus before closing the doors.

That September the very difficult decision was made to disband by December 31, 2000. We were heartbroken. Thankfully my friends did not let me down. Even though that announcement had been made, work was being done behind the scenes to save the organization. Someone had been given the opportunity to assume leadership—me. Although I felt completely inadequate, I wanted very much to see Project Linus continue. We had done so much good, and I felt strongly that we were all duty bound to do everything possible to continue our mission. From that time forward I have been unable to spend as much time quilting and making blankets as I would have liked, but I am confident that I have played an important role in bringing many more blankets to children who need a warm snuggly hug. In late October 2000, after many months of discussions about how the changes would take place, I received a phone call from Laurie, our Project Linus treasurer. The board members felt they were ready to make the change and turn over their beloved organization to new management. Everything was falling into place. But I knew that I could not do this alone. Besides the fact that it would be logistically impossible, there are also many state and federal rules that dictate the organization and administration of nonprofit organizations. Coincidentally, my family was

moving again, this time to Central Illinois. My mind kept going back to my friend, Mary Balagna, whom I had met the previous summer at Project Linus Conference. She also lived in Central Illinois. It was time to make a phone call to my friend.

It is my extraordinary good fortune to work with amazing people to create and nurture an organization that has exceeded all of our expectations. It has truly been a family affair. From my husband—who is willing to do anything great and small—to my two sons who don't remember a life without Project Linus, our lives are entangled with Project Linus in a way that has blessed our family. I have also had the privilege of working with thousands of chapter coordinators and volunteers who daily demonstrate their love for children and dedication to Project Linus. They are compassionate and unselfish in ways that still surprise me every day. But one of my greatest blessings came that day when Mary took a gigantic leap of faith with me and agreed to help me try to save Project Linus. My life has been enriched by our friendship and partnership. I am a better person because of knowing her and learning from her.

I know that my mother could not have known the impact of her teachings as she simply tried to be a good mom, but she set me on a path to know the deep fulfillment that comes from serving others, cherishing good friends and loving family. I not only remember who I am because of her, I am that person because of her. Mom—I love you and miss you. This is for you.

Carol Babbitt

Designed and pieced by Mary Balagna
Quilted by Linda Strate

Life's Ups and Downs

Although we can't always control real-life ups and downs, you can control the ups and downs of this bargello-style quilt.

FINISHED QUILT SIZE
39½" x 46½" (100.3 x 118.1 cm)

SEAM ALLOWANCE
¼" (6 mm)

Note: This quilt is a "theme quilt." Select one fabric of a particular theme (i.e., music, trucks, cars, ballet, bugs, butterflies, tools, etc.). Large-scale prints work well for this fabric. This will be your "theme print fabric." Then, add six coordinating fabrics and arrange them in order as desired. Finish it off with a contrasting solid or tone-on-tone color border and bind.

MATERIALS
- Basic Supplies & Tools, page 11
- **Theme print:** ¼ yard (.2 m) of fabric
- **Strips:** ¼ yard (.2 m) of six coordinating fabrics (fabrics A–F)
- **Borders:** 1 yard (.9 m) solid or tone-on-tone contrasting fabric
- **Backing:** 1⅓ yards (1.2 m) of backing fabric
- **Binding:** ½ yard (.5 m) of fabric
- **Batting:** 44" x 50" (111.8 x 127 cm)

Cutting
From theme print:
Cut one strip, 6½" (16.5 cm) x WOF (width of fabric).

From each fabric A and E:
Cut one strip, 3½" (8.9 cm) x WOF.

Cut one strip, 3" (7.6 cm) x WOF.

From fabric B:
Cut one strip, 2½" (6.4 cm) x WOF.

Cut one strip, 2" (5.1 cm) x WOF.

From fabric C:
Cut one strip, 1½" (3.8 cm) x WOF.

Cut one strip, 3½" (8.9 cm) x WOF.

From fabric D:
Cut one strip, 2½" (6.4 cm) x WOF.

Cut one strip, 5" (12.7 cm) x WOF.

From fabric F:
Cut one strip, 4½" (11.4 cm) x WOF.

Cut one strip, 2½" (6.4 cm) x WOF.

From border fabric:
Cut three strips, 2½" (6.4 cm) x WOF.

Cut two strips, 10" (25.4 cm) x WOF.

From binding fabric:
Cut five strips, 2½" (6.4 cm) x WOF.

DIFFICULTY

Dear Project Linus,

After my friend died in an automobile accident my life was so confused. I began to go into a downward slope. I even cried because I needed air in my car tires. I had lost all faith and hope in life when our school nurse approached me with a Project Linus blanket. I felt better. The idea that someone had done something so special for me that didn't even know me made me feel so relieved. I thank you for sending me a blanket and showing that you cared.

The blanket always reminds me of the good times I shared with my friend. I hope your organization has brought other kids as much comfort as it has brought me. Thank you again for your blanket and your concerns.

On the back of the card, from his mother:
Thanks for the kindness of your organization. When the school nurse called me to pick up my son, she told me she had given him a Linus blanket. When I picked him up, my 16-year-old son was in the nurse's office holding the blanket. Tears were shed by all. My son was a pallbearer for his good friend. He has had a tough time dealing with the loss. But thanks to your project, some comfort has been found. Your blanket can be found on his bed and he sleeps with it each night.

Thanks for caring!!

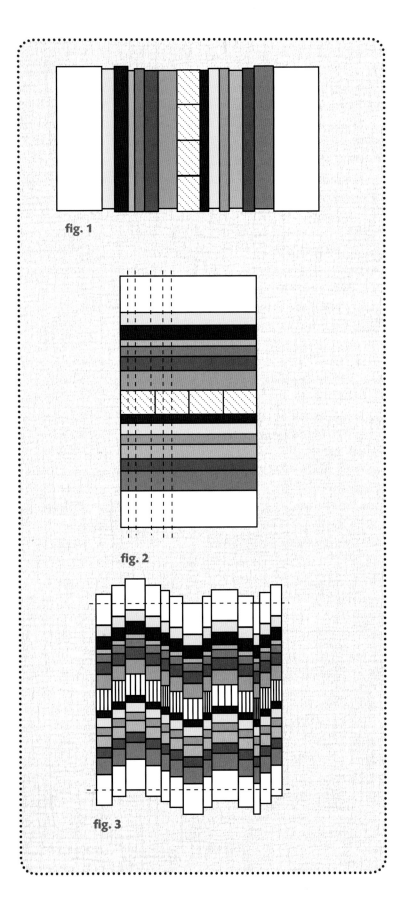

fig. 1

fig. 2

fig. 3

Assembly
Creating the Strips

1 Number the theme and fabric A–F strips in sewing order, randomly placing strips 1–6 and 7–12 on each side of the theme print. Add the 10-inch (25.4 cm) border strips to begin and end the strips. For the best results, use contrasting prints positioned side by side.

2 Sew the fabric strips together, alternately sewing the strips from top to bottom and then bottom to top to keep the joined pieces from curving as each new strip is added (**Fig. 1**). Press seams in one direction.

3 Trim the uneven edges by making a straight cut across the top and bottom of the pieced fabric.

4 Flip the pieced fabric so that strips lie horizontally across your work surface. Cut the fabric into 13 units as follows (**Fig. 2**):

Unit 1: 3½ inches (8.9 cm) wide

Unit 2: 3 inches (7.6 cm) wide

Unit 3: 4½ inches (11.4 cm) wide

Unit 4: 3½ inches (8.9 cm) wide

Unit 5: 2 inches (5.1 cm) wide

Unit 6: 3 inches (7.6 cm) wide

Unit 7: 4½ inches (11.4 cm) wide

Unit 8: 2 inches (5.1 cm) wide

Unit 9: 6 inches (15.2 cm) wide

Unit 10: 3½ inches (8.9 cm) wide

Unit 11: 1½ inches (3.8 cm) wide

Unit 12: 2½ inches (6.4 cm) wide

Unit 13: 3½ inches (8.9 cm) wide (size approximate)

Assembling the Quilt Top

5 Arrange the units side by side, as shown, placing some strips higher and some lower at varying increments (**Fig. 3**). Do not measure; just place them where you feel they look best. This will give the quilt top the "up and down" look. Label the strips in numerical order and then sew them together. Press the seams in one direction.

6 Trim the uneven edges by cutting off 2 inches (5.1 cm) above the highest strip and below the lowest strip (**Fig. 3**).

Adding Borders

7 Measure the length of the side edges and piece together the border strips to make two vertical border strips.

8 Add borders as follows: Sew a pieced border strip to each side edge of the quilt top. Then sew the remaining border strips to the top and bottom edges of the quilt.

Finishing the Quilt

9 Create the backing, following the instructions on page 15. Layer the backing, batting, and quilt top to make a quilt sandwich and baste the layers together.

10 Quilt as desired.

11 Sew the binding strips together and bind the edge of the quilt, following the Binding instructions, page 17.

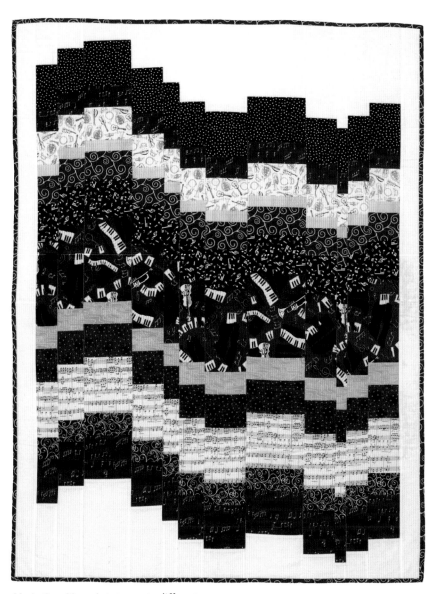

Variation: Use prints to create different themes for your quilt. In this case, we used music-themed fabrics for a sophisticated look.

Designed and pieced by Mary Balagna

Quilted by Althea Warner

Pocket Full of Posies

Stitch up this bright and cheerful quilt: It's a snap with snowball blocks, nine-patch blocks, and a few simple appliquéd hearts and flowers sprinkled here and there.

FINISHED QUILT SIZE
36" x 48" (91.4 x 121.9 cm)

FINISHED BLOCK SIZE
6" square (15.2 cm)

SEAM ALLOWANCE
¼" (6 mm)

MATERIALS
- Basic Supplies & Tools, page 11
- Pocket Full of Posies Templates, page 119
- **Fabric A:** ½ yard (.5 m) of tone-on-tone blue fabric
- **Fabric B:** ½ yard (.5 m) of tone-on-tone green fabric
- **Fabric C, border:** ¾ yard (.7 m) of tone-on-tone yellow fabric
- **Background fabric:** 1 yard (.9 m) of tone-on-tone white fabric
- **Hearts:** 8 assorted pink or red fabric scraps, each at least 6" square (15.2 cm)
- **Flowers:** 9 assorted fabric scraps, each at least 6" square (15.2 cm)
- **Flower centers:** Assorted yellow fabric scraps
- **Backing:** 1½ yards (1.4 m) of backing fabric
- **Binding:** ½ yard (.5 m) of binding fabric

- **Batting:** 40" x 52" (101.6 x 132 cm)
- Paper-backed fusible web, 3 yards (2.7 m)

Cutting

From each fabric A and B:
Cut five strips each, 2½" (6.4 cm) x WOF (width of fabric).

From fabric A and B strips, cut two full strips and half of a third strip into 2½" (6.4 cm) squares—34 total squares of each fabric.

From fabric C, border:
Cut two strips, 2½" (6.4 cm) x WOF.

Cut four strips, 3½" (8.9 cm) x WOF for the border.

From background fabric:
Cut five strips, 2½" (6.4 cm) x WOF.

Cut three strips, 6½" (16.5 cm) x WOF.

Cut the three strips into seventeen 6½" (16.5 cm) squares.

From heart fabrics:
Cut eight 6" (15.2 cm) squares.

From flower fabrics:
Cut nine 6" (15.2 cm) squares.

From binding fabric:
Cut six strips, 2½" (6.4 cm) x WOF.

DIFFICULTY

Assembly

Creating the Snowball Blocks

1 Draw a pencil line diagonally from corner to corner on the wrong side of each fabric A and B square. The line will serve as your stitching guide.

2 Place a green marked B square in the opposite corners of each 6½-inch (16.5 cm) white background square, right sides together. Stitch along the pencil line in each corner, trim the seam allowances to ¼ inch (6 mm), and discard the corner pieces. Repeat with the blue marked A squares—17 total Snowball Blocks. Press the seams toward corner triangles (**Fig. 1**).

3 Photocopy or trace the Pocket Full of Posies Templates on page 119. Using the templates, cut eight hearts from the heart fabric and nine flowers and flower centers from the flower fabrics. Appliqué the shapes in the centers of the 17 Snowball Blocks, following the Appliqué instructions on page 12.

Creating the Nine-Patch Blocks

4 Piece together strip sets as shown (**Fig. 2**) using the remaining 2½-inch (6.4 cm) x WOF strips of fabric A, B, C, and the background fabric. You will need the following strip sets for each block:

• 2½ WOF strips of Strip Set BWG (about 80 inches [203.2 cm])

• 1¼ WOF strips of Strip Set WYW (about 45 inches [114.3 cm])

5 Cut the strip sets into 2½-inch (6.4 cm) units, creating 36 of Strip Set BWG and 18 of Strip Set WYW (**Fig. 2**).

6 Join together two of Strip Set BWG and one of Strip Set WYW as shown for each block—18 total Nine-Patch Blocks. Press the seams toward the center strips (**Fig. 3**).

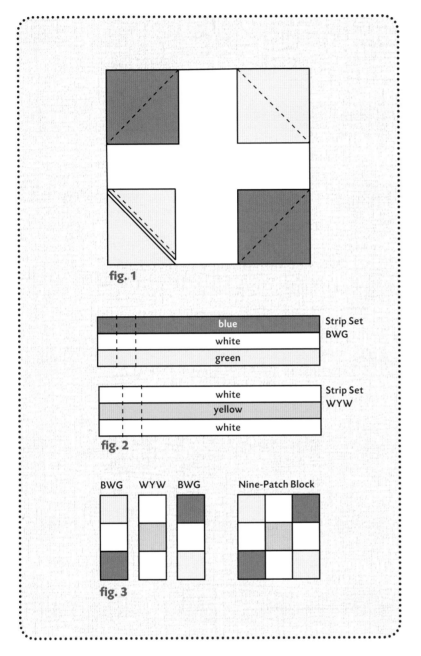

fig. 1

Strip Set
BWG

blue
white
green

Strip Set
WYW

white
yellow
white

fig. 2

BWG   WYW   BWG   Nine-Patch Block

fig. 3

Assembling the Quilt Top

7 Join together the 35 blocks as desired to create seven rows of five blocks each, alternating heart and flower appliqué blocks. Press the seams toward the appliqué blocks.

Adding Borders

8 Add borders as follows: Sew a border strip to each side edge of the quilt top. Then sew the remaining strips to the top and bottom edges of the quilt.

Finishing the Quilt

9 Create the backing, following the instructions on page 15. Layer the backing, batting, and quilt top to make a quilt sandwich and baste the layers together.

10 Quilt as desired.

11 Sew the binding strips together and bind the edge of the quilt, following the Binding instructions, page 17.

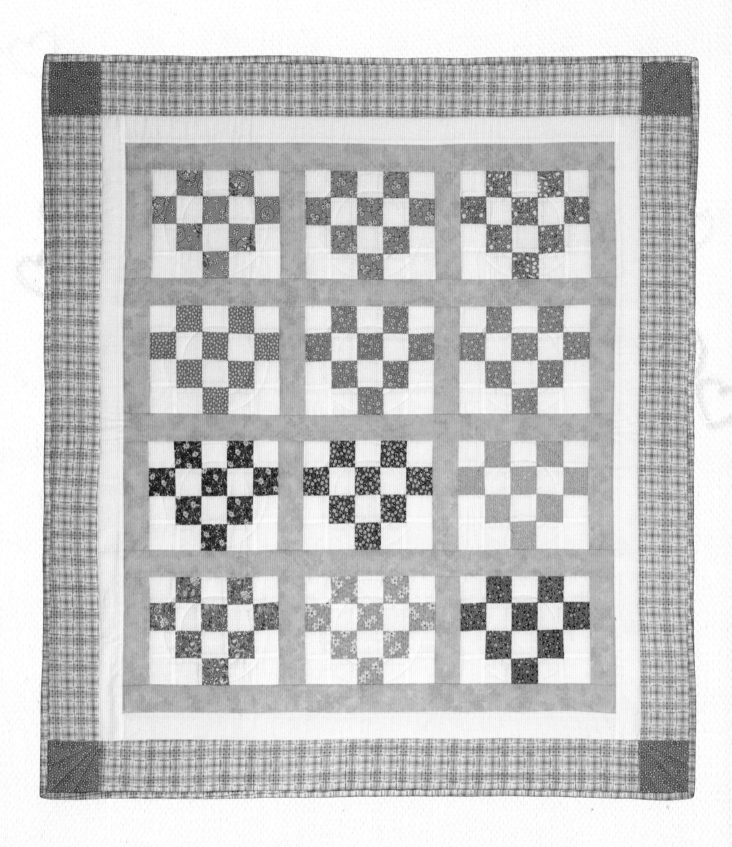

Designed, pieced, and quilted by Mary Balagna

Follow Your Heart

We've always believed that when you follow your heart, only good things can happen!

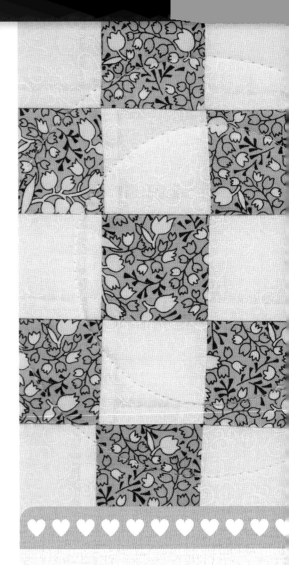

FINISHED QUILT SIZE
38" x 41½" (96.5 x 105.4 cm)

FINISHED BLOCK SIZE
6" x 7½" (15.2 x 19 cm)

SEAM ALLOWANCE
¼" (6 mm)

MATERIALS
- Basic Supplies & Tools, page 11
- **Hearts:** 12 fat quarters (45.7 x 55.9 cm) of fabric
- **Inner border #1, sashing:** ½ yard (.5 m) of fabric
- **Inner border #2, background fabric for hearts:** 1 yard (.9 m) of fabric
- **Outer border:** ½ yard (.5 m) of fabric
- **Corner squares:** 4 fabric scraps, each at least 3½" square (8.9 cm)
- **Backing:** 1¼ yards (1.1 m) of backing fabric
- **Binding:** ½ yard (.5 m) of fabric
- **Batting:** 42" x 45" (106.7 x 114.3 cm)

DIFFICULTY

Cutting
From fat quarter fabrics:
Cut one strip, 2" (5.1 cm) x WOF (width of fabric), from each fat quarter.

Cut strips into eight 2" (5.1 cm) squares—96 total squares.

From inner border #1, sashing fabric:
Cut eight strips, 2" (5.1 cm) x WOF. Set aside five strips for horizontal sashing and the horizontal inner border #1 strips.

Cut three of the strips into 16 strips, 2" x 6½" (5.1 x 16.5 cm), for vertical sashing.

From inner border #2, heart background fabric:
Cut 11 strips, 2" (5.1 cm) x WOF. Set aside four strips for the inner border #2 strips.

Cut the seven remaining strips into 2" (5.1 cm) squares, for heart background squares—144 total squares.

From outer border fabric:
Cut four strips, 3½" (8.9 cm) x WOF.

From corner square fabric scraps:
Cut four 3½" (8.9 cm) squares.

From binding fabric:
Cut five strips, 2½" (6.4 cm) x WOF.

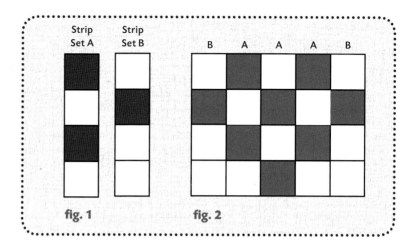

| Strip Set A | Strip Set B | | B | A | A | A | B |
| fig. 1 | | fig. 2 | | | | | |

Assembly

Creating the Blocks

1 Piece together heart squares and background squares as shown (**Fig. 1**). You will need the following strip sets for each block:

- Three of Strip Set A.

- Two of Strip Set B.

2 Join the five strip sets together to create a heart block as shown, pressing each strip set in the opposite direction of the adjacent set (**Fig. 2**). Repeat to make all 12 heart blocks.

Assembling the Quilt Top

3 Join together the blocks and the vertical sashing strips as shown to create four horizontal rows of three blocks each.

4 Cut the five horizontal sashing strips to 29 inches (73.7 cm) and join the horizontal rows together with these strips.

Note: Always measure the size of the finished blocks and adjust the length of the sashing strips accordingly, as needed.

Adding Borders

5 Add inner borders as follows: Sew an inner border #2 strip to each side edge of the quilt top. Then sew the remaining inner border #2 strips to the top and bottom edges of the quilt.

6 Add outer borders following the Adding a Border with Corner Squares instructions, page 14.

Finishing the Quilt

7 Create the backing, following the instructions on page 15. Layer the backing, batting, and quilt top to make a quilt sandwich and baste the layers together.

8 Quilt as desired.

9 Sew the binding strips together and bind the edge of the quilt, following the Binding instructions, page 17.

Lattice of Love

Using this "split a square" strip-piecing technique and a combination of scraps and solid strips, you can create a beautiful yet simple patchwork lattice quilt top, filled with love.

FINISHED QUILT SIZE
39" x 50" (99 x 127 cm)

FINISHED BLOCK SIZE
5½" square (14 cm)

SEAM ALLOWANCE
¼" (6 mm)

MATERIALS
- Basic Supplies & Tools, page 11
- **Fabrics for behind the lattice:** 48 assorted fabric scraps, each at least 6" square (15.2 cm)
- **Lattice, border:** 1½ yards (1.4 m) of tone-on-tone solid fabric
- **Backing:** 1¾ yards (1.6 m) of backing fabric
- **Binding:** ½ yard (.5 m) of binding fabric
- **Batting:** 42" x 54" (106.7 x 137.2 cm)

- **Optional:** Masking tape, 1" (2.5 cm) wide
- **Optional:** Ruler square, 6" square (15.2 cm)

Cutting

From assorted fabric scraps:
Cut forty-eight 6" (15.2 cm) squares.

From solid fabric:
Cut 10 strips, 2½" (6.4 cm) x WOF (width of fabric), for lattice.

Cut five strips, 3" (7.6 cm) x WOF, for horizontal borders; side borders will be pieced.

From binding fabric:
Cut five strips, 2½" (6.4 cm) x WOF.

DIFFICULTY

Dear Project Linus,

My name is Christine, and I am 17 years old. I was in a coma from a drug overdose on my 17th birthday, and the doctors told my parents I might die. The nurses gave me this blanket that somebody from your organization made for me, and I absolutely love it! It represents a time in my life that God helped me get through and survive. I appreciate it so much, and it gave me so much comfort in the hospital. Thank you, and I think your organization is amazing and a blessing. The hospital even let me take it home. It gives me great comfort and reminds of what I went through. God bless.

Christine

Designed by Shirley Hughes

Pieced and quilted by Mary Balagna

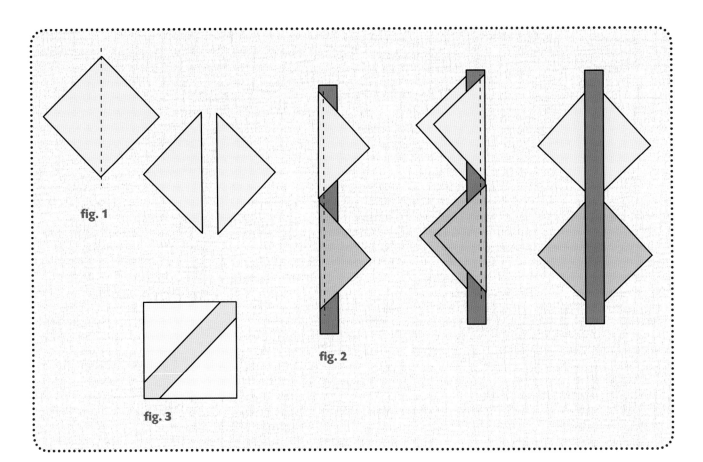

fig. 1

fig. 2

fig. 3

Assembly
Creating the Blocks

1 Cut the assorted fabric scrap squares diagonally from corner to corner, creating 96 half-square triangles. Keep the two stacks of half-square triangles in order: Stack A and Stack B, with 48 triangles per stack (**Fig. 1**).

2 Begin chain-piecing with Stack A, sewing the diagonal edge of the triangles onto a lattice strip. Press the seams toward the strip. Then start at the top of the strip and sew a matching triangle to the other side of the strip. Five pairs of triangles will fit on one strip. Press the seams toward the triangles (**Fig. 2**).

3 Cut apart the pairs, then trim the blocks to 6 inches square (15.2 cm) (**Fig. 3**). Make sure the lattice is centered down the middle of the square. Create 48 total blocks.

Note: To make a perfectly centered block, place a strip of the masking tape on each side of the diagonal, 45° center line of the 6-inch (15.2 cm) square ruler. As you cut the squares, position the ruler so that the masking tape completely covers the center lattice strip.

Assembling the Quilt Top

4 Join together the blocks as desired to create eight horizontal rows of six blocks each.

Adding Borders

5 Measure the length of the side edges and piece together leftover lattice fabric to make two vertical border strips.

6 Add borders as follows: Sew a pieced border strip to each vertical side edge of the quilt top. Then sew the remaining border strips to the top and bottom edges of the quilt.

Finishing the Quilt

7 Create the backing, following the instructions on page 15. Layer the backing, batting, and quilt top to make a quilt sandwich and baste the layers together.

8 Quilt as desired.

9 Sew the binding strips together and bind the edge of the quilt, following the Binding instructions, page 17.

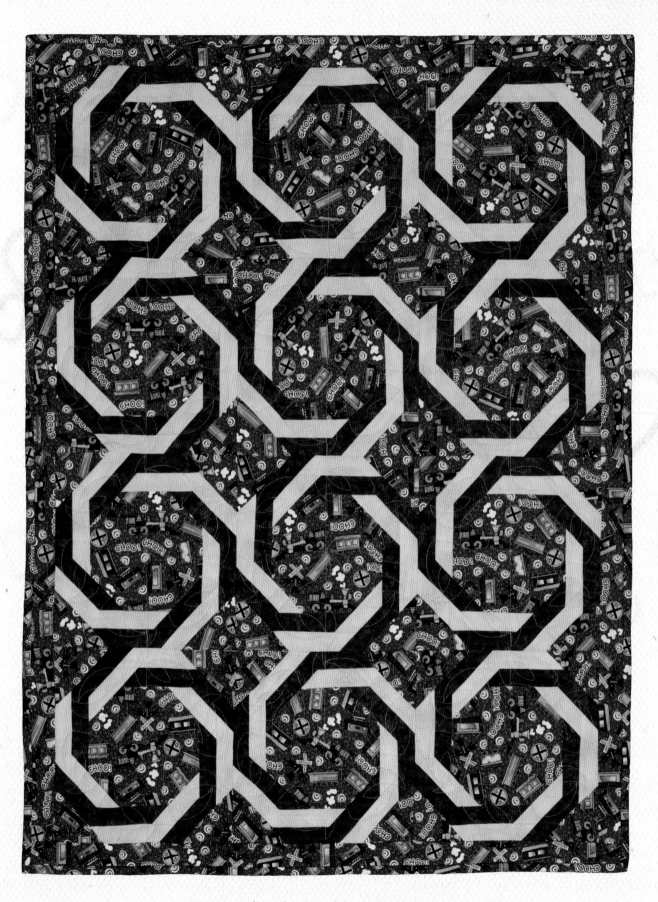

Designed and pieced by Mary Balagna

Quilted by Ron and Kay Gerard

Ring Toss

It's carnival time! This clever quilt gives the illusion of woven patchwork circles, each surrounding a novelty fabric center.

FINISHED QUILT SIZE
34½" x 45" (87.6 x 114.3 cm)

FINISHED BLOCK SIZE
10½" square (26.7 cm) unfinished

SEAM ALLOWANCE
¼" (6 mm)

MATERIALS
- Basic Supplies & Tools, page 11
- **Ring fabric A:** ¾ yard (.7 m) of tone-on-tone fabric
- **Ring fabric B:** ¾ yard (.7 m) of contrasting tone-on-tone fabric
- **Ring centers, border:** 1½ yards (1.4 m) of novelty fabric
- **Backing:** 1½ yards (1.4 m) of backing fabric
- **Binding:** ½ yard (.5 m) of binding fabric
- **Batting:** 39" x 49" (99.1 x 124.5 cm)

DIFFICULTY

Cutting

From each ring fabric:
Cut two strips, 6" (15.2 cm) x WOF (width of fabric).

Cut strips into 1½" x 6" (3.8 x 15.2 cm) strips—48 strips of each fabric.

Cut two strips, 7" (17.8 cm) x WOF.

Cut strips into 1½" x 7" (3.8 x 17.8 cm) strips—48 strips of each fabric.

From the novelty fabric:
Cut two strips, 7" (17.8 cm) x WOF.

Cut strips into twelve 7" (17.8 cm) squares.

Cut three strips, 4½" (11.4 cm) x WOF.

Cut strips into twenty-four 4½" (11.4 cm) squares.

Cut 4½" squares in half diagonally from corner to corner—48 total half-square triangles.

Cut six strips, 2" (5.1 cm) x WOF, for borders.

From the binding fabric:
Cut six strips, 2½" (6.4 cm) x WOF.

Dear Project Linus,

My phone rang with a frantic phone call from my daughter. Andrew, my three-year-old great grandson, had fallen out of a shopping cart, hit the back of his head on the cement floor, and was on his way to the emergency room. As I ran into the ER, there sat Andrew opening a beautiful quilt donated by Project Linus. Andrew, the quilt, and Mom were transferred to a more specialized hospital where all three went through CT scanning together. Fortunately, Andrew was able to return home several hours later with only a slight fracture at the base of his skull and a mild concussion. His quilt now sleeps with him every night. I for one can tell you what a difference Project Linus makes to a traumatized child, not to mention the parents, grandparents, and great grandparents. My heartfelt thanks to everyone who has contributed to Project Linus in the past and to those who will in the future. Project Linus is a wonderful organization, and I sincerely thank all of you who make it possible. You truly do make a wonderful difference.

My sincere thanks,
Andrew's great-grandmother

Assembly
Creating the Blocks

1 Measure 2 inches (5.1 cm) from each corner of a 7-inch (17.8 cm) novelty fabric square. Make a small pencil mark on the horizontal and vertical side of the fabric square. Position a ruler on the diagonal, using the pencil marks as a guide, and cut off the corners of the square, creating an octagon (**Fig. 1**). Repeat with the remaining novelty squares—12 total octagons.

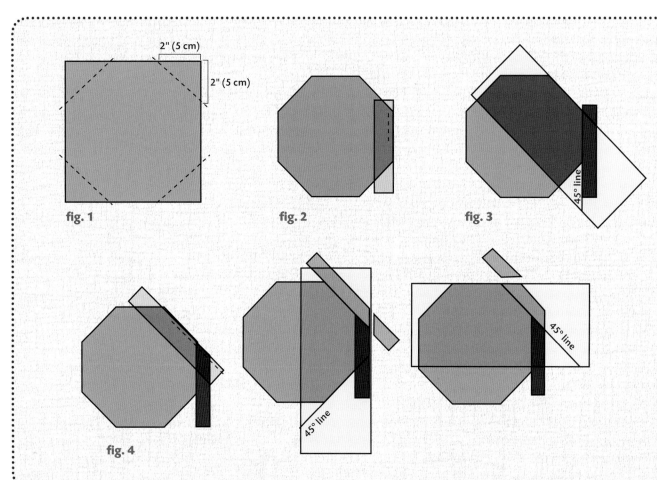

2" (5 cm)

2" (5 cm)

fig. 1

fig. 2

45° line

fig. 3

fig. 4

45° line

45° line

Round 1:

2 Align a 6-inch (15.2 cm) strip of ring fabric A (strip #1) on one side of an octagon so that the strip extends about ½ inch (1.3 cm) above the corner of the octagon. Sew halfway down the side of the octagon for this strip only (**Fig. 2**). Press the seam toward the strip.

3 Place the 45° line of your ruler along the cut edge of the octagon and the edge of the ruler along the adjacent cut edge of the octagon, as shown. Trim off the top corner of the newly attached strip. This method will give you an accurate cut, allowing the octagon to maintain its shape (**Fig. 3**).

4 Moving in a counter-clockwise direction around the octagon, attach strips to six octagon edges (pieces #2–#7), alternating ring fabrics A and B. Always trim after pressing the newly attached strip (**Fig. 4**).

5 Complete the first ring by folding the unsewn half of strip #1 out of the way, and attach a strip #8 to the cut edge in the same manner as strips #2–#7. Press the seam allowance and trim excess fabric. Then finish sewing the rest of the strip #1 seam over strip #8.

6 Repeat steps 1–5 to create 12 total ring blocks with one round of piecing.

Round 2:

7 Add the 7-inch (17.8 cm) fabric A and B strips to the edges of the octagon, following the instructions for Round 1 and alternating colors (**Fig 5**). Begin by sewing half of strip #1 to the side of the octagon so that you will be able to attach strip #1 to strip #8 at the end of the round.

8 Sew a half-square triangle to each corner of the ring block and trim to measure 11 inches square (27.9 cm) (**Fig. 6**).

Assembling the Quilt Top

9 Join together the blocks in four rows of three blocks each. Join the rows together.

Adding Borders

10 Add borders as follows: Sew a border strip to each side edge of the quilt top, trimming and piecing to size. Then sew the horizontal border strips to the top and bottom edges of the quilt.

Finishing the Quilt

11 Create the backing, following the instructions on page 15. Layer the backing, batting, and quilt top to make a quilt sandwich and baste the layers together.

12 Quilt as desired.

13 Sew the binding strips together and bind the edge of the quilt, following the Binding instructions, page 17.

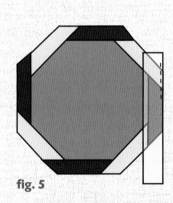

fig. 5

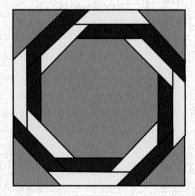

fig. 6

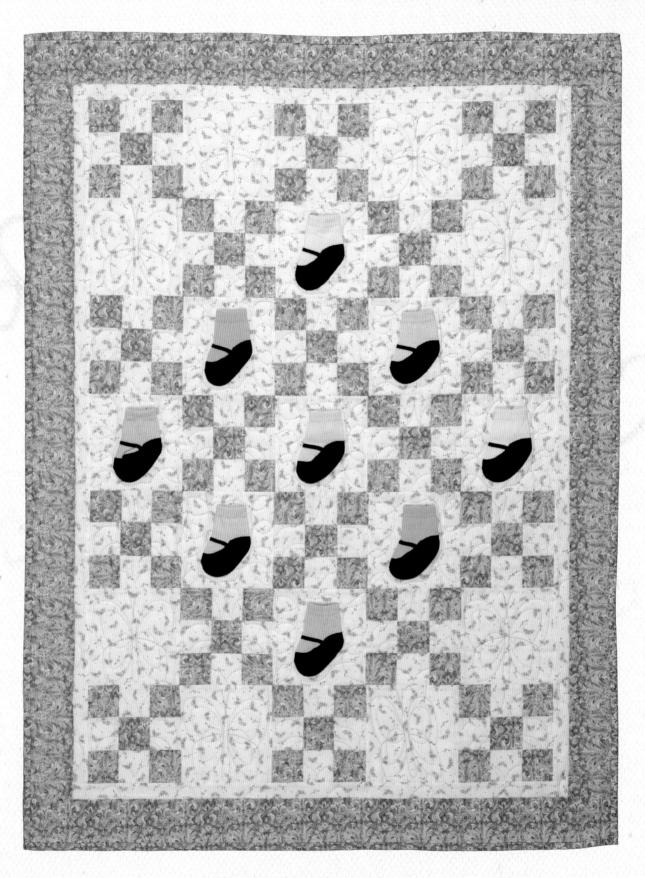

Designed by Elzora Channer

Pieced by Mary Balagna   Quilted by Ron and Kay Gerard

Sock It To Me!

This quilt combines a simple Irish chain pattern and fun appliqued socks, great for stowing toys, supplies, games, or even special notes for a special child.

FINISHED QUILT SIZE
38" x 50" (96.5 x 127 cm)

FINISHED BLOCK SIZE
6" square (15.2 cm)

SEAM ALLOWANCE
¼" (6 mm)

MATERIALS
- Basic Supplies & Tools, page 11
- **Chain, outer border, binding:** 1¼ yards (1.1 m) of fabric
- **Background, inner border:** 1¼ yards (1.1 m) of fabric
- **Backing:** 1½ yards (1.4 m) of backing fabric
- **Batting:** 42" x 54" (106.7 x 137.2cm)
- 9 baby socks

Cutting
From chain fabric:
Cut 11 strips, 2½" (6.4 cm) x WOF (width of fabric); set aside five strips for binding.

Cut five strips, 3½" (8.9 cm) x WOF, for outer border.

From background fabric:
Cut five strips, 2½" (6.4 cm) x WOF.

Cut four strips, 1½" (3.8 cm) x WOF, for inner border.

Cut three strips, 6½" (16.5 cm) x WOF.

Cut the 6½" (16.5 cm) strips into seventeen 6½" (16.5 cm) squares.

DIFFICULTY

Share Project Linus updates and news on Facebook and Twitter.

Dear Project Linus,

Our daughter, age four, was transported in an ambulance to the hospital. While I was trying to console her, a pink butterfly blanket was given to my daughter, who was trying to be so brave but had just a few tears in her eyes. When she saw that blanket and was told her it was "just for her" and that she could keep it, her eyes lit up like a Christmas tree!

I have to tell you that she sleeps with that blanket every night now. Although that morning is a very bad memory for us all, the pink butterfly blanket made it all better for my daughter. So please accept this letter as our most sincere thanks to you for making such a beautiful blanket, as it made everything okay. You and the organization have touched our lives in a very special way, and we will never forget it.

Thank you!

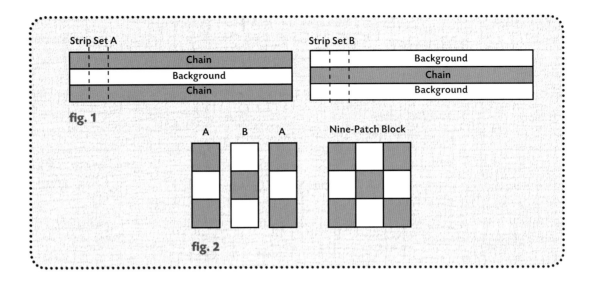

Strip Set A

| Chain |
| Background |
| Chain |

Strip Set B

| Background |
| Chain |
| Background |

fig. 1

A B A

Nine-Patch Block

fig. 2

Assembly

Creating the Nine-Patch Blocks

1 Piece together chain fabric strips (Ch) and background strips (Bk) as shown (**Fig. 1**). You will need the following strip sets for each block:

• 2½ WOF strips of Strip Set A (Ch-Bk-Ch)

• 1¼ WOF strips of Strip Set B (Bk-Ch-Bk)

2 Cut each of the strip sets into 2½-inch-wide (6.4 cm) units—36 of Strip Set A and 18 of Strip Set B (**Fig. 2**).

3 Piece together two of Strip Set A and one of Strip Set B, creating a Nine-Patch Block. Repeat to create 18 total Nine-Patch Blocks (**Fig. 2**). Press the seams toward the center strips.

Creating the Sock Blocks

4 Center and pin a sock on each of nine 6½-inch (16.5 cm) background squares.

5 Machine or hand stitch each sock in place, leaving the top of each sock open so that they can be used as pockets.

Assembling the Quilt Top

6 Join together the Nine-Patch Blocks, Sock Blocks, and the remaining background squares to create seven rows of five blocks each, alternate Nine-Patch Blocks and 6½-inch (16.5 cm) blocks as desired. Press the seams toward the 6½-inch (16.5 cm) blocks.

Adding Borders

7 Add inner borders as follows: Sew an inner border strip to each side edge of the quilt top. Then sew the remaining inner border strips to the top and bottom of the quilt.

8 Sew an outer border strip to each side edge of the quilt top, trimming and piecing to size. Then sew the horizontal outer border strips to the top and bottom of the quilt.

Finishing the Quilt

9 Create the backing, following the instructions on page 15. Layer the backing, batting, and quilt top to make a quilt sandwich and baste the layers together.

10 Quilt as desired.

11 Sew the binding strips together and bind the edge of the quilt, following the Binding instructions, page 17.

It's Strip to Be Square

Select a novelty fabric and two coordinating tone-on-tone solids, and turn your pieced strips into this quick-to-make quilt.

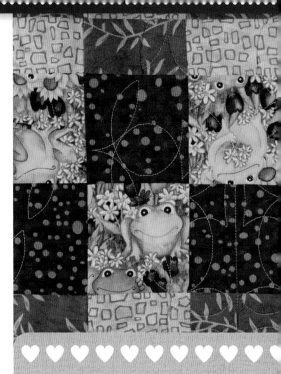

FINISHED QUILT SIZE
41" x 54" (104.1 x 137.1 cm)

FINISHED BLOCK A SIZE
3" x 6" (7.6 x 15.2 cm)

FINISHED BLOCK B SIZE
6" square (15.2 cm)

SEAM ALLOWANCE
¼" (6 mm)

MATERIALS
- Basic Supplies & Tools, page 11
- **Block A color #1:** ½ yard (.5 m) of novelty fabric
- **Block A color #2 , border:** 1 yard (.9 m) of coordinating fabric A
- **Block B color #1:** ½ yard (.5 m) of coordinating fabric B
- **Block B color #2:** ½ yard (.5 m) of coordinating fabric C
- **Backing:** 1¾ yards (1.6 m) of backing fabric

- **Binding:** ½ yard (.5 m) of binding fabric
- **Batting:** 45" x 59" (114.3 x 149.9 cm)

Cutting

From novelty fabric:
Cut five strips, 3½" (8.9 cm) x WOF (width of fabric).

From coordinating fabric A:
Cut five strips, 3½" (8.9 cm) x WOF.

Cut six strips, 2½" (6.4 cm) x WOF, for the border.

From coordinating fabric B:
Cut four strips, 3½" (8.9 cm) x WOF.

From coordinating fabric C:
Cut four strips, 3½" (8.9 cm) x WOF.

From binding fabric:
Cut five strips, 2½" (6.4 cm) x WOF.

DIFFICULTY

Dear Project Linus,
My child was in the hospital for surgery. She was given a beautiful Project Linus blanket. I wanted you to know how much we appreciated the time and effort that went into making this blanket. We have gotten so many compliments on the beautiful workmanship and the pretty colors. Everybody asked her for it, and she tells them "no way, it's mine!" Thanks for making my child happy. It's nice to know that there are people who don't even know my child, but care about her. We are very grateful to the maker of the blanket and for Project Linus.

Designed and pieced by Mary Balagna

Quilted by Ron and Kay Gerard

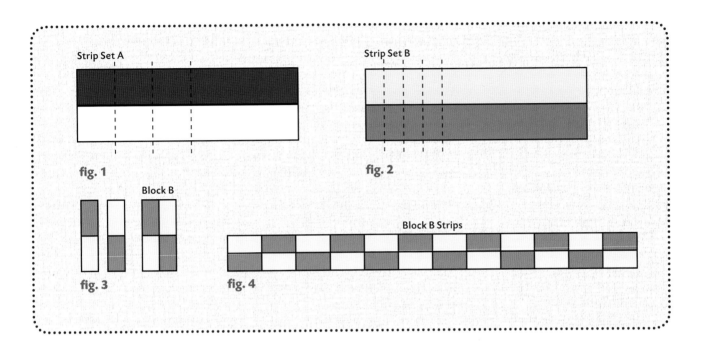

fig. 1

fig. 2

Block B

fig. 3

Block B Strips

fig. 4

Assembly

Creating the Strips

1 Sew each novelty fabric strip to a 3½-inch (8.9 cm) fabric A strip, creating five WOF strips of Strip Set A. Press the seams toward the novelty fabric.

2 Cut 12 vertical strips, 3½ x 6½ inches (8.9 x 16.5 cm), from each Strip Set A—60 total rectangles (Fig. 1).

3 Sew each fabric B strip to a fabric C strip, creating four WOF strips of Strip Set B. Press the seams toward the darker fabric.

4 Cut 18 vertical strips, 2 x 6½ inches (5.1 x 16.5 cm), from each Strip Set B—72 total rectangles (Fig. 2).

Creating the Blocks

5 Piece together two Strip Set A rectangles, creating a four-patch Block A, 6½ inches square (16.5 cm). Make 30 total blocks.

6 Piece together two Strip Set B rectangles as shown, creating a four-patch Block B, 6½ x 4 inches (16.5 x 10.2 cm). Make 36 total blocks (Fig. 3).

Assembling the Quilt Top

7 Join together six A blocks to create a strip. Make five total strips.

8 Join together six B blocks to create a strip. Make six total strips (Fig. 4).

9 Piece together the quilt top by alternating Block B strips and Block A strips, beginning and ending with a Block B strip.

Adding Borders

10 Add borders as follows: Sew a border strip to each side edge of the quilt top. Then sew the remaining border strips to the top and bottom of the quilt.

Finishing the Quilt

11 Create the backing, following the instructions on page 15. Layer the backing, batting, and quilt top to make a quilt sandwich and baste the layers together.

12 Quilt as desired.

13 Sew the binding strips together and bind the edge of the quilt, following the Binding instructions, page 17.

Designed by Kim Hazlett

Pieced by Mary Balagna   Quilted by Ron and Kay Gerard

It's a Jungle Out There

We all know it's a jungle out there, but it's smooth sailing with this fun and easy quilt, with a too-cute fussy-cut feature print.

FINISHED QUILT SIZE
45¾" square (116.2 cm)

FINISHED BLOCK SIZE
8" square (20.3 cm)

SEAM ALLOWANCE
¼" (6 mm)

MATERIALS
- Basic Supplies & Tools, page 11
- **Novelty fabric squares:** 9 scraps of novelty print fabric, each featured print at least 6⅛" square (15.6 cm)
- **Accent fabric:** 8 fat quarters (45.7 x 55.9 cm) of fabric
- **Background, outer border fabric:** 1¼ yards (1.1 m) of neutral fabric
- **Backing:** 2¾ yards (2.5 m) of backing fabric
- **Binding:** ½ yard (.5 m) of binding fabric
- **Batting:** 50" square (127 cm)

Note: If the featured print in your novelty squares is smaller than 6⅛" square (15.6 cm), add coordinating fabric strips around the print to achieve the desired size. In the sample quilt, jungle animals were cut from a quilt panel.

DIFFICULTY

Cutting

From novelty fabric:
Fussy cut nine 6⅛" (15.6 cm) squares.

From all fat quarters:
Cut one strip, 5¼" x 18" (13.3 x 45.7 cm), from each fat quarter.

Cut two 5¼" (13.3 cm) squares from six of the strips.

Cut three 5¼" (13.3. cm) squares from the remaining two strips.

Cut all the squares diagonally from corner to corner—36 total triangles for Square-in-a-Square blocks.

Cut two strips, 3" x 18" (7.6 x 45.7 cm), from each fabric.

Cut three rectangles, 3" x 6½" (7.6 x 16.5 cm), from each fabric, plus one additional rectangle from two fat quarter fabrics for inner border rectangles.

From one fat quarter fabric (yellow):
Cut one strip, 1½" x 18" (3.8 x 45.7 cm).

Cut four 1½" (3.8 cm) squares from the strip—4 total center squares for Alternate Blocks.

From four fat quarter fabrics:
Cut three strips, 2" x 18" (5.1 x 45.7 cm).

Cut six rectangles, 2" x 4" (5.1 x 10.2 cm), from two of the strips— 24 total wide Alternate Block pieces.

Cut six rectangles, 2½" x 2" (6.4 x 5.1 cm), from the remaining strip— 24 total thin Alternate Block pieces.

From background fabric:
Cut two strips, 2½" (6.4 cm) x WOF (width of fabric).

Cut twenty-four 2½" (6.4 cm) squares from the 2½" (6.4 cm) strips for Alternate Blocks.

Cut two strips, 1½" (3.8 cm) x WOF.

Cut 16 rectangles, 1½" x 4" (3.8 x 10.2 cm), from the 1½" (3.8 cm) strips for Alternate Blocks.

Cut one strip, 8½" (21.6 cm) x WOF.

Cut four 8½" (21.6 cm) squares from the strip.

Cut the squares diagonally from corner to corner, four triangles per square—16 total side triangles.

Cut one strip, 6¾" (17.1 cm) x WOF.

Cut two 6¾" (17.1 cm) squares from the strip.

Cut the squares diagonally from corner to corner—4 total corner triangles.

Cut five strips, 4" (10.2 cm) x WOF, for outer border.

From binding fabric:
Cut five strips, 2½" (6.4 cm) x WOF.

Assembly
Creating the Square-in-a-Square Blocks

1 Randomly piece a fat quarter triangle to each side of the fussy-cut novelty fabric squares. Press the seams toward the triangles and trim the squares to 8½ inches (21.6 cm)—nine total Square-in-a-Square blocks **(Fig. 1)**.

Creating the Alternate Blocks

2 Create six corner units from the rectangles cut from the four selected tone-on-tone fat quarters. Sew a 2½-inch (6.4 cm) background square to a colored 2½ x 2-inch (6.4 x 5.1 cm) rectangle. Press the seam toward the colored rectangle **(Fig. 2)**, and then sew a 2 x 4-inch (5.1 x 10.2 cm) rectangle of the same color to the side of the pieced unit, creating a corner unit. Press the seams toward the colored rectangle **(Fig. 2)**. Repeat to create six corner units from each selected fabric—24 total corner units.

Invite your local chapter to host a booth at your guild quilt show.

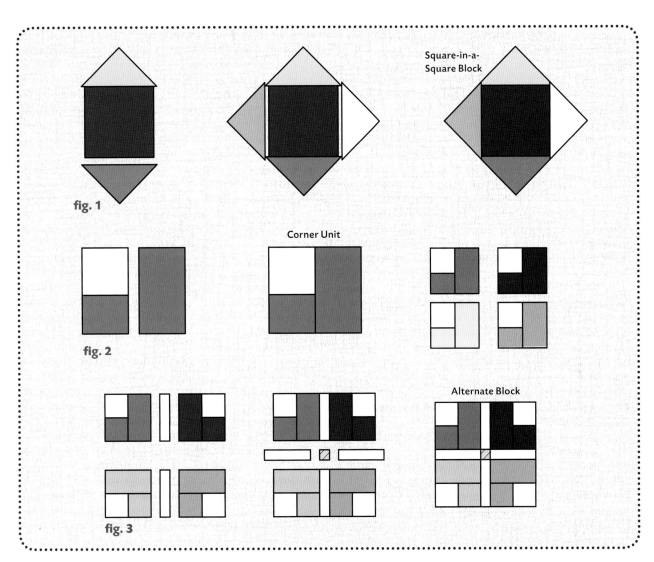

fig. 1

Square-in-a-Square Block

Corner Unit

fig. 2

Alternate Block

fig. 3

3 Assemble four corner units (one of each color), a center square, and four background rectangles to create an Alternate Block as follows: Sew a corner unit to each long side of two background rectangles as shown. Press the seams toward the background rectangle. Then sew an unpieced background rectangle to the sides of the center square in the same way. Press the seams toward the background rectangle. Join the corner square strips and the center square strip as shown (**Fig. 3**).

4 Repeat step 3 to create four identical Alternate Blocks. Eight corner units remain, two of each color.

Creating the Side Triangle Units

5 Sew a background side triangle to one side of a corner unit. Press the seam toward the corner unit. Then sew another background side triangle to the adjacent side of the pieced corner unit (**Fig. 4**).

6 Repeat step 5 to create eight total Side Triangle Units. These units will be oversized. You will trim these when you trim the sides of the quilt top.

Assembling the Quilt Top

7 Join together the blocks and the Side Triangle Units on a diagonal to create five diagonal columns. Begin sewing the rows on the diagonal with the corners. Press the seams toward the Alternate Blocks and Side Triangle Units as you go, sewing the corner triangles last (**Fig. 5**). Press the seams toward the corner triangles.

Note: *Be sure to pay attention to the placement of the side triangles, matching the corner units in the Side Triangle Units with the corner units in the Alternate Blocks.*

8 Trim the sides of the quilt top, leaving a ¼-inch (6 mm) seam allowance from the Square-in-a-Square block points.

Adding Borders

9 Add inner borders as follows: Piece together six 3 x 6½-inch (7.6 x 16.5 cm) colored inner border rectangles for the vertical borders and seven 3 x 6½-inch (7.6 x 16.5 cm) colored inner border rectangles for the horizontal borders. Measure the sides of the quilt and trim the border strips to size, cutting off an equal measurement off each end of each strip.

10 Sew inner border strips to each vertical side edge of the quilt top. Measure the top and bottom of the quilt, and cut off an equal measurement from each end of each pieced horizontal inner border strip. Then sew the strips to the top and bottom edges of the quilt.

11 Add outer border strips in the same way, piecing as needed.

Finishing the Quilt

12 Create the backing, following the instructions on page 15. Layer the backing, batting, and quilt top to make a quilt sandwich and baste the layers together.

13 Quilt as desired.

14 Sew the binding strips together and bind the edge of the quilt, following the Binding instructions, page 17.

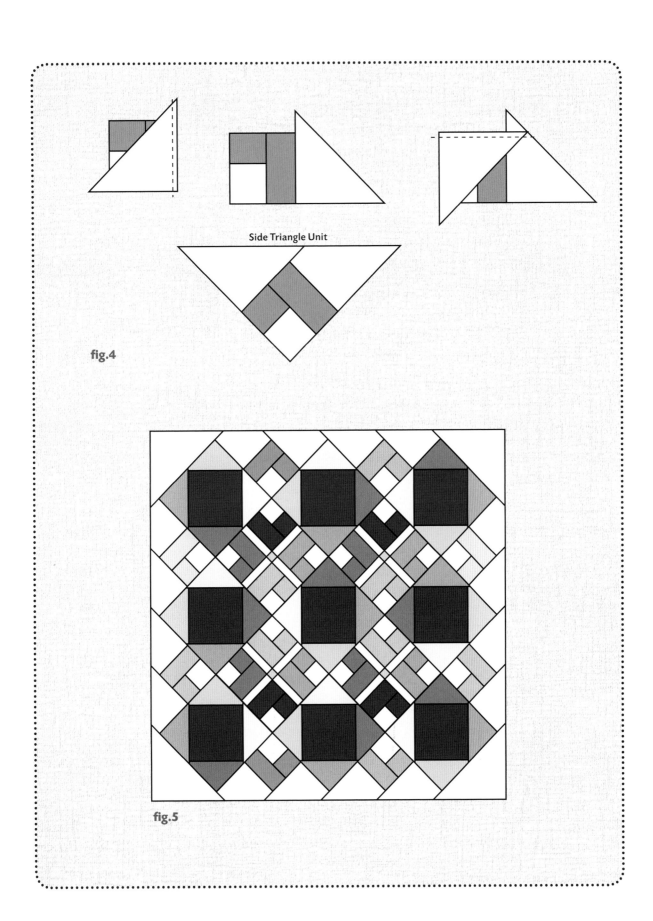

Side Triangle Unit

fig.4

fig.5

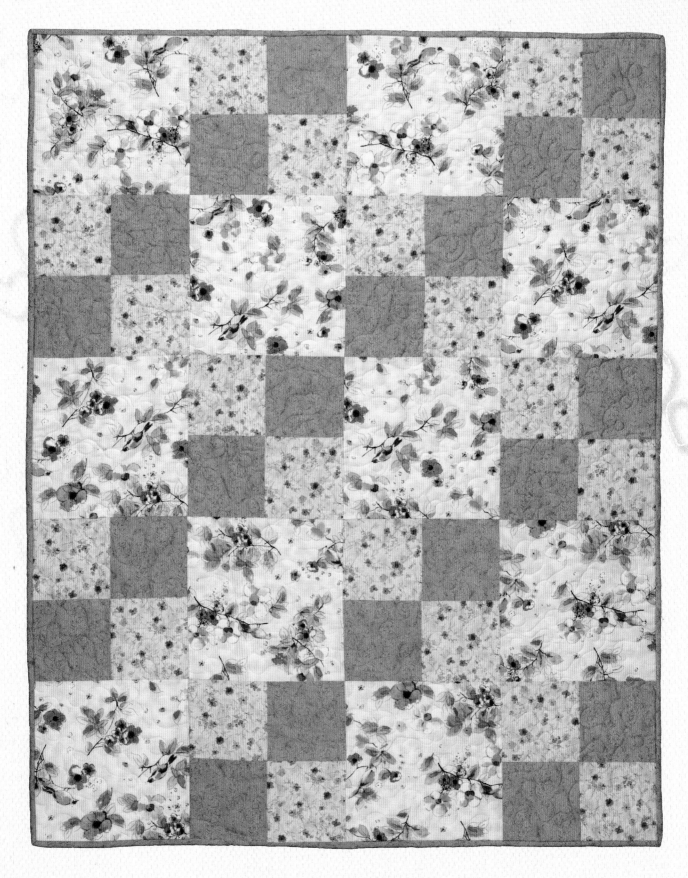

Designed by Cheryl Hughes

Pieced and quilted by Mary Balagna

All Patched Up

A quick-and-easy pattern for beginning and veteran quilters alike, this quilt is great for experimenting with large- and small-scale prints. And the matching tote bag (page 100) is too cute to resist.

FINISHED QUILT SIZE
44" x 55" (111.8 x 139.7 cm)

FINISHED BLOCK SIZE
11" square (27.9 cm)

SEAM ALLOWANCE
¼" (6 mm)

MATERIALS
Basic Supplies & Tools, page 11

- **Four-patch blocks:** ½ yard (.5 m) of coordinating small-scale print fabric A
- **Four-patch blocks:** ½ yard (.5 m) of coordinating tone-on-tone solid fabric B
- **Background fabric for squares:** 1⅓ yards (1.2 m) of large-scale print fabric C
- **Backing:** 1¾ yards (1.6 m) of backing fabric
- **Binding:** ½ yard (.5 m) of binding fabric

DIFFICULTY

- **Batting:** 48" x 59" (121.9 x 149.9 cm)

Note: If the width of the backing fabric is less than 44" (111.8 cm), you will need to horizontally piece the backing with an additional 2½ yards (2.3 m) of fabric. Excess fabric can be used for binding.

Cutting

From four-patch squares fabric A:
Cut three strips, 6" (15.2 cm) x WOF (width of fabric).

From four-patch squares fabric B:
Cut three strips, 6" (15.2 cm) x WOF.

From background squares fabric C:
Cut four strips, 11½" (29.2 cm) x WOF.

Cut ten 11½" (29.2 cm) squares.

After cutting the ten 11½" (29.2 cm) squares, set aside an 11½" x 20" (29.2 x 50.8 cm) strip for the pillowcase tote.

From binding fabric
Cut the fabric into five strips, 2½" (6.4 cm) x WOF.

Dear Project Linus blanketeers,
Although our daughter was born five weeks early, we felt very grateful that she was born without any complications and was able to go home just as any baby would.

Just when we thought we had enough surprises, when she was 2 months old we discovered that she needed to have surgery for a relatively common stomach issue called pyloric stenosis. In order to "rule out any serious issues" I (her mom) was advised to take her to the hospital for an ultrasound. Since I didn't anticipate anything other than a quick and painless procedure, I took her while my husband was at work. Shortly after the procedure I was told that I should contact my husband because she was going to need to have surgery that very day. You can imagine my shock. We are first-time parents with a new baby and there we were scared and helpless in the hospital with our precious little baby waiting for her to go in for surgery.

Obviously we didn't even have a bag packed for her, so while she was in surgery we began to make a list of things that my

(Continued on p. 98)

♥ 97 ♥

Assembly
Creating the Block

1 Sew each fabric A strip to a fabric B strip as shown, creating three A/B strip sets. Press the seams toward the darker fabric (**Fig. 1**).

2 Cut each strip set into rectangles, 6 x 11½ inches (15.2 x 29.2 cm)—20 two-patch rectangles (**Fig. 1**).

3 Piece together 2 two-patch rectangles as shown, creating a four-patch block, 11½-inch square (29.2 cm). Repeat to create 10 blocks (**Fig. 2**).

Assembling the Quilt Top

4 Piece together the quilt top by alternating background fabric squares (C) and four-patch blocks in a five-row grid.

(Continued from p. 97)

husband would pick up from our house afterwards.

When they brought our sweetheart back, she was covered in tubes. Among all of the white hospital lines was a beautiful quilt. I asked the nurse where it came from and she told me that it was donated by Project Linus. I remember being so touched. That is the best word that can describe how I felt. It was like some invisible person was there with us comforting us. The nurse asked me if I would like for her to get a different blanket but I immediately answered, "no thank you."

I didn't want to change a thing about the precious gift that was so lovingly wrapped around my baby after she came out of her surgery. Our daughter is nine months old now and perfectly healthy and happy! I have seen the "Project Linus" label on it many times and thought to myself how much I would love to know who took the time to hand make it for my baby. Please know that your loving kindness has truly touched our hearts, and I will make sure that our daughter knows the awesome story behind her blue blanket one day. Thank you!

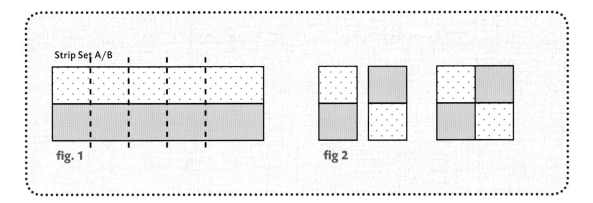

Strip Set A/B

fig. 1

fig 2

Finishing the Quilt

5 Create the backing, following the instructions on page 15. Layer the backing, batting, and quilt top to make a quilt sandwich and baste the layers together.

6 Quilt as desired.

7 Sew the binding strips together and bind the edges of the quilt, following the Binding instructions, page 17.

Most children receive a Project Linus blanket through a local hospital, shelter, or other agency. If you know a child in crisis who will not likely get a Project Linus blanket from one of these facilities, please contact the chapter most convenient to the child's location.

Variation: Switch colors and fabrics to create this quilt for a boy recipient. The "checkered flags" are perfect with the race car novelty fabric.

All Patched Up Quilt Tote

Designed and assembled by Mary Balagna

FINISHED TOTE SIZE
15½" x 25" (39.4 x 63.5 cm)

SEAM ALLOWANCE
¼" (6 mm)

MATERIALS
Basic Supplies & Tools, page 11

- **Tote cuff:** ¼ yard (.2 m) of coordinating small-scale print fabric A
- **Tote:** ⅔ yard (.6 m) of tone-on-tone solid fabric B
- **Casing:** 1 piece of accent fabric, at least 2" x 33" (5.1 x 83.8 cm)
- **Pocket:** 1 piece of background fabric C, at least 11½" x 20" (29.2 x 50.8 cm) (leftover from the quilt)
- **Cording:** 1½ yards (1.4 m) of cording, ¼" (6 mm) wide
- **Safety pin**

Cutting
From tote cuff fabric A:
Cut one rectangle, 7" x 33" (17.8 x 8.38 cm).

From tote fabric B:
Cut one rectangle, 22" x 33" (55.9 x 83.8 cm).

From casing fabric:
Cut one strip of fabric for the casing, 2" x 33" (5.1 x 83.8 cm).

From pocket background fabric C:
Cut one rectangle, 11½" x 20" (29.2 x 50.8 cm).

DIFFICULTY

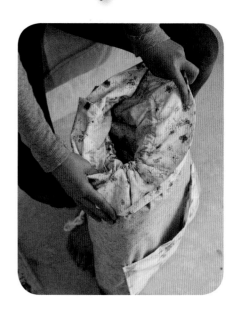

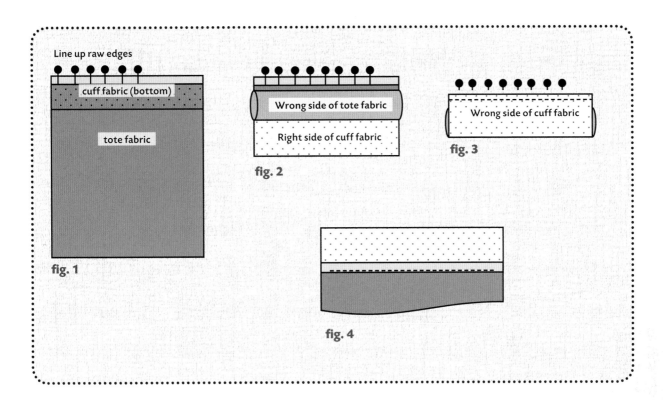

Line up raw edges

cuff fabric (bottom)

tote fabric

fig. 1

Wrong side of tote fabric

Right side of cuff fabric

fig. 2

Wrong side of cuff fabric

fig. 3

fig. 4

Assembly

Creating the Cuff and Casing

1 Fold the casing strip in half and press, creating a 1-inch-wide (2.5 cm) folded strip.

2 Fold the cuff fabric A in half and press, creating a 3½-inch-wide (8.9 cm) strip. Unfold the strip.

3 Layer the tote fabric B on top of the cuff fabric A, right sides facing up. Pin the folded casing strip on top of both fabrics with the open selvage edges at the top, lining up the raw edges and trimming if needed (**Fig. 1**).

4 Pin in place across top edge. Starting at the bottom of the tote roll the fabric up to the top, about 1 to 2 inches (2.5 to 5.1 cm) from the pinned edge, creating a tube. Do not roll the cuff fabric with the tote fabric (**Fig. 2**).

5 Fold the cuff fabric A up and over the tube and re-pin all layers together (**Fig. 3**). Sew along the pinned edge and remove pins. Turn the cuff right side out, pulling the tote fabric out of the tube. Press.

6 Topstitch the free edge of the casing strip, beginning and ending with a backstitch approximately 1 inch (2.5 cm) from each edge (**Fig. 4**).

Creating the Pocket

7 Fold the pocket fabric in half, right sides together, creating a 10-inch-wide (25.4 cm) rectangle. Sew along each 10-inch (25.4 cm) side, leaving the bottom edge open. Turn and press.

8 Sew a double-stitched line across the top of the pocket, about 1½" (3.8 cm) from the top edge.

9 Center the pocket on the tote, lining up the open edge of the pocket with the bottom edge of the tote. Topstitch the vertical sides of pocket in place, backstitching at the top edges to secure.

Assembling the Tote

10 Fold the tote in half lengthwise, right sides together, to center the seam opposite the pocket. Sew closed the long open edge of the tote using a zigzag stitch. Then sew closed the bottom of the tote using a serger or zigzag stitch to prevent fraying. Turn the tote right side out and press.

11 Feed the cording through the casing using the safety pin. Tie the ends of the cording to prevent raveling and then tie the ends of the cord together.

Designed by Merlene Sanborn

Pieced and quilted by Mary Balagna

Sweet Simplicity

A sweet novelty fabric, some coordinating solids, and an assortment of detachable tactile toys around the edges create the perfect recipe for a sweet baby quilt.

FINISHED QUILT SIZE
41" x 51" (104.1 x 129.5 cm)

SEAM ALLOWANCE
¼" (6 mm)

MATERIALS
- Basic Supplies & Tools, page 11
- Toy Templates, page 121
- **Long strips:** 1 yard (.9 m) of novelty fabric
- **Pieced strips:** ½ yard (.5 m) each of two coordinating tone-on-tone solid fabrics
- **Backing:** 1½ yards (1.4 m) of backing fabric
- **Binding:** ½ yard (.5 m) of binding fabric
- **Batting:** 45" x 55" (114.3 x 139.7 cm)
- 2 yards (1.8 m) grosgrain ribbon, 1" (2.5 cm) wide
- **Toy fronts:** 8 scraps of assorted textured fabrics, each at least 6½" square (16.5 cm)
- **Toy backs:** 8 scraps of cotton fabric, each at least 6½" square (16.5 cm)
- Polyester fiberfill for stuffing toys
- 8 plastic links

Note: For the toy fronts, choose fabrics with an array of textures, including cotton, corduroy, chenille, fake fur, satin, flannel, artificial leather, or suede.

Cutting
From the novelty fabric:
Cut nine strips, 4" (10.2 cm) x WOF (width of fabric).

From each solid fabric:
Cut six strips, 2½" (6.4 cm) x WOF.

Cut strips into 9" x 2½" (22.9 x 6.4 cm) strips—25 strips from each fabric.

From binding fabric:
Cut five strips, 2½" (6.4 cm) x WOF.

From ribbon:
Cut 16 lengths, 4" (10.2 cm) long.

DIFFICULTY

Assembly

Creating the Strips

1 Piece together 9 x 2½-inch (22.9 x 6.4 cm) solid fabric strips as shown, alternating colors to create five pieced strips of five units each—10 total pieced strips. Press the seams in one direction (**Fig. 1**).

Assembling the Quilt

2 Join the 10 pieced strips and the nine novelty fabric strips, beginning and ending with a pieced strip. Alternately sew the strips from top to bottom and then bottom to top to keep joined pieces from curving as each new strip is added. Press the seams toward the novelty strips and trim any uneven edges (**Fig. 2**).

Finishing the Quilt

3 Create the backing, following the instructions on page 15. Layer the backing, batting, and quilt top to make a quilt sandwich and baste the layers together.

4 Quilt as desired.

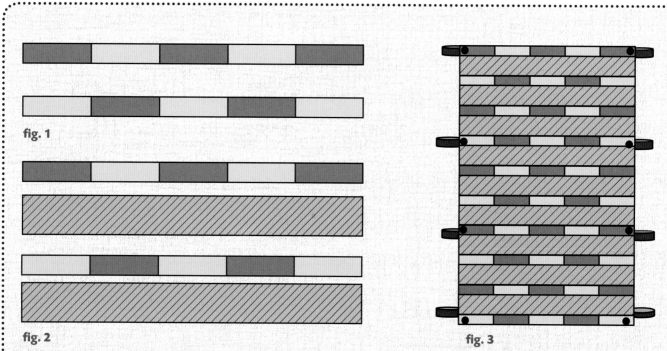

fig. 1

fig. 2

fig. 3

5 Sew the binding strips together. When attaching the binding to the quilt (following the Binding instructions, page 17) fold each length of ribbon in half to create a loop and stitch it into the binding so that it is displayed as desired on the top side of the quilt **(Fig. 3)**.

Making the Toys

6 Photocopy or trace the Toy Templates on page 121 onto a sturdy template material (cardstock, cardboard, template plastic, etc.). Using the templates, trace each shape on the wrong side of the scraps of fabric for the toy backs, but do not cut out the shapes.

7 Pin each traced toy front fabric to a corresponding toy back fabric, right sides together. Fold a length of ribbon and pin it in place between the layers, with the ribbon's raw edges toward the seam. Stitch around each toy, leaving an opening approximately 2 inches (5.1 cm) for turning **(Fig. 4)**.

8 Cut out each toy, leaving a ¼-inch (6 mm) seam allowance. Trim corners or clip curves as needed, turn, and stuff with fiberfill. Hand stitch the opening closed.

9 Secure the toys to the quilt using the plastic links to join loops.

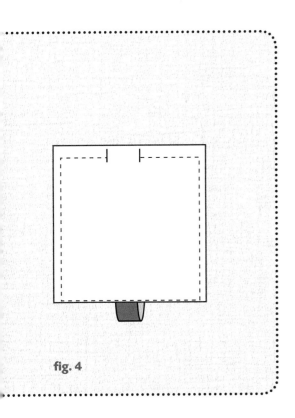

fig. 4

Designed, pieced, and quilted by Mary Balagna

Turtles Hiding in the Marsh

Take a traditional curved block, add a head and a tail, and you've created a sweet little patchwork turtle.

FINISHED QUILT SIZE
49" x 62" (124.5 x 157.5 cm)

FINISHED BLOCK SIZE
13" square (33 cm)

SEAM ALLOWANCE
¼" (6 mm)

MATERIALS
- Basic Supplies & Tools, page 11
- Turtle Templates, page 120
- Foundation Marsh Block Pattern, page 120
- **Turtles:** 6 fat quarters (45.7 x 55.9 cm) of "turtle"-colored fabrics
- **Marsh, outer border fabric:** 25 jelly roll fabric strips, 2½" x 44" (6.4 x 111.8 cm).
- **Block backgrounds:** 1¾ yards (1.6 m) of fabric
- **Corner fabric for turtle blocks:** ¾ yard (.7 m) or fabric
- **Corner fabric for marsh blocks:** ¾ yard (.7 m) of fabric
- **Inner border, corner squares, binding:** 1 yard (.9 m) of fabric
- **Backing:** 3 yards (2.7 m) of backing fabric
- **Batting:** 53" x 66" (134.6 x 167.6 cm)
- Paper for foundation piecing
- Glue sticks

DIFFICULTY

Notes: 12" (30.5 cm) squares of turtle and background fabrics make two turtles. You can use a variety of green or brown fabrics or one turtle fabric for all six turtles and cut one strip, 3" (7.6 cm) x WOF (width of fabric).

Backing for this quilt must be horizontally pieced.

Cutting

From each turtle fat quarter fabric:
Using templates A and B, cut two A pieces and two B pieces from each fat quarter.

Cut two rectangles, 2" x 3" (5.1 x 7.6 cm), and one 3" (7.6 cm) square from each fabric for heads and tails—twelve total rectangles and six squares.

From the marsh fabrics:
Cut the twenty-five 2½" x 44" (6.4 x 111.8 cm) fabric strips in half. (Eighteen of the half strips will be used for marsh squares and the remaining half strips will be used for the outer border.)

Select 18 strips from the marsh jelly roll fabrics:
Cut two rectangles, 2½" x 4" (6.4 x 10.2 cm), for each block—12 rectangles: pieces #2 and #2R.

Cut two rectangles, 2½" x 6½" (6.4 x 16.5 cm), for each block—12 rectangles: piece #4 and #4R.

Cut two rectangles, 2½" x 8½" (6.4 x 21.6 cm), for each block—12 rectangles: pieces #6 and #6R.

For one marsh foundation pieced block you will have six blades in three different colors: small, medium, and large—pieces #2, #2R, #4, #4R, and #6, #6R.

From block background fabric:
Using templates A and B, cut 12 of each shape.

Cut 12 rectangles, 2½" x 5" (6.4 x 12.7 cm): pieces #1 and #1R.

Cut 12 rectangles, 2½" x 6" (6.4 x 15.2 cm): pieces #3 and #3R.

Cut 12 rectangles, 2½" x 7" (6.4 x 17.8 cm): pieces #5 and #5R.

Cut 12 rectangles, 2½ x 9" (6.4 x 22.9 cm): pieces #7 and #7R.

Cut 12 strips, 1½" x 7½" (3.8 x 19 cm), for marsh block border strips.

Cut 12 strips, 1½" x 9½" (3.8 x 24.1 cm), for marsh block border strips.

From each corner fabric:
Cut three strips, 7¼" (18.4 cm) x WOF—6 total strips.

Cut strips into 7¼" (18.4 cm) squares.

Cut squares diagonally from corner to corner—24 total corner triangles.

From inner border, corner squares, and binding fabric:
Cut eight strips, 1½" (3.8 cm) x WOF, for inner border.

Cut one strip, 4" (10.2 cm) x WOF.

Cut strip into four 4" (10.2 cm) squares, for corner squares.

Cut six strips, 2½" (6.4 cm) x WOF, for binding.

Assembly
Creating the Turtle Blocks

You will make six Turtle Blocks.

You will need four A pieces (two turtle and two background), four B pieces (two turtle and two background), two turtle head pieces, one tail piece, and four corner triangles to create each block.

1 Place two turtle head pieces right sides together. Trace the Turtle Head Template onto the stacked turtle head pieces. Sew along the curved marked line, leaving the bottom edge open and backstitching at the beginning and ending of the seam. Trim ⅛ inch (3 mm) around the head, clip curves, turn, and press **(Fig. 1)**.

2 Match and sew together the curved edges of a turtle A piece and background B piece. Insert and center the finished head in the seam, pin, and sew. Press the seam toward the background piece **(Fig. 2)**.

3 Repeat steps 1 and 2 to create six turtle head sections.

4 Match and sew together the curved edges of a background A piece and a turtle B piece. Press the seam toward the turtle piece. Repeat to make two total turtle shell sections for each block—12 total shell sections **(Fig. 3)**.

5 Fold and press the turtle tail piece, right sides together, as shown **(Fig. 4)**.

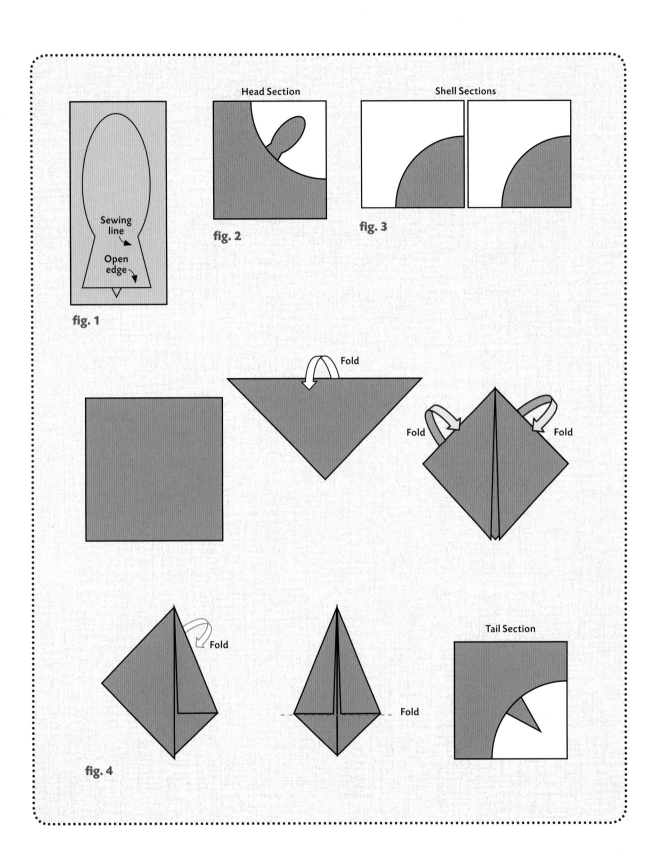

Head Section

Shell Sections

Sewing line

Open edge

fig. 1

fig. 2

fig. 3

Fold

Fold

Fold

Fold

Fold

Tail Section

fig. 4

Creating the Marsh Blocks

11 Photocopy or trace the Foundation Marsh Block Pattern onto the foundation paper. Make 12 copies, six regular blocks and six reversed blocks.

12 Paper piece each Marsh Block in numerical order, following the Paper Piecing instructions on page 13.

13 Sew together a regular block and a reversed block, creating a 7½-inch (19 cm) unfinished block.

14 Sew a 1½ x 7½-inch (3.8 x 19 cm) background strip to opposite sides of the block. Press the seams toward the background strips. Then sew a 1½ x 9½-inch (3.8 x 24.1 cm) background strip to the remaining two sides of the block. Press the seams toward the background strips.

15 Sew a corner triangle to each side of the Marsh Block. Press the seams toward the corner triangles. Trim the block to 13¼ inches square (33.7 cm).

16 Repeat steps 13–15 to assemble all six Marsh Blocks.

6 Match and sew together the curved edges of a turtle A piece and a background B piece. Insert and center the finished tail in the seam, pin, and sew. Press the seam toward the background piece and trim excess fabric (**Fig. 5**).

7 Repeat steps 5 and 6 to create six turtle tail sections.

8 Piece together a shell section and head section as shown. Press the seam toward the head. Then piece together a tail section and shell section. Press the seam toward the tail. Piece together the joined pairs as shown and press (**Fig. 5**).

9 Sew a corner triangle to each side of the Turtle Block. Press the seams toward the corner triangles. Trim the block to 13¼ inches square (33.7 cm).

10 Repeat steps 8 and 9 to assemble all six Turtle Blocks.

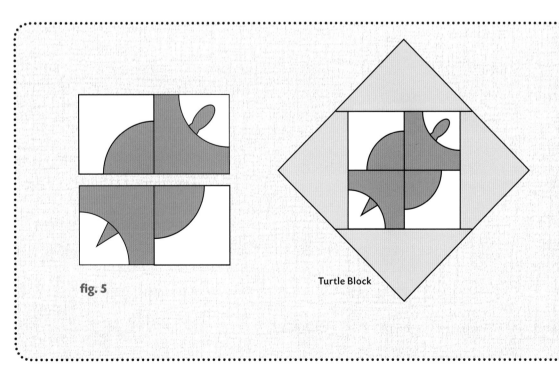

fig. 5

Turtle Block

Assembling the Quilt Top

17 Join the blocks into four rows of three blocks each, alternating Turtle Blocks and Marsh Blocks.

Adding the Border

18 Add inner borders as follows: Sew an inner border strip to each side edge of the quilt top. Then sew the remaining inner border strips to the top and bottom of the quilt.

19 Sew together 21 cut jelly roll strips, 2½ x 22 inches (6.4 x 55.9 cm). Cut two border strips from the pieced fabric, 4 x 42 inches (10.2 x 106.7 cm) for outer border strips. Measure the top and bottom edges of the quilt top and trim the horizontal border strips to size (**Fig. 6**).

20 Sew six cut jelly roll strips to the remaining pieced fabric. Cut two border strips, 4 x 54 inches (10.2 x 137.2 cm). Measure the side edges of the quilt top and trim the vertical border strips to size (**Fig. 7**).

21 Add outer borders following the Adding a Border with Corner Squares instructions, page 14.

Finishing the Quilt

22 Create the backing, following the instructions on page 15. Layer the backing, batting, and quilt top to make a quilt sandwich and baste the layers together.

23 Quilt as desired.

24 Sew the binding strips together and bind the edge of the quilt, following the Binding instructions, page 17.

Dear Project Linus,

Project Linus has been a blessing to our youth. So often, small ones come to the hospital traumatized by illness or injury. They are thrown into a strange environment totally devoid of all things that are familiar to them. We are able to offer the gift of a comfort-giving quilt and say, "This is yours. You can take it with you when you go home." Often this turns a frightened, tear-stained frown into a bright smile.

Some children try to put up a facade but let emotions flow about receiving a Linus blanket. Parents are comforted when they see their child hug a new Linus blanket. Just today, an eight-year-old boy came in for emergency surgery. Trying to maintain the "tough guy" facade, he told of sighting his first deer in the woods. We were able to offer him a camouflage quilt, perfect for this little hunter.

May God richly bless the hands that patiently sew smiles together.

Sincerely, Hospital Chaplain

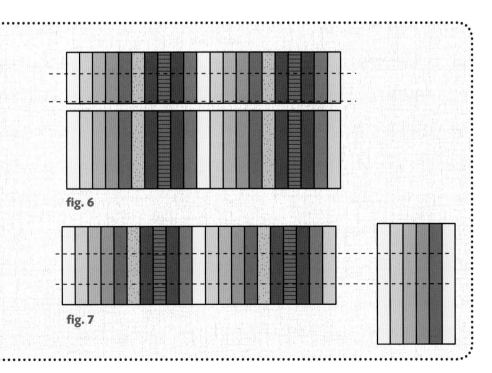

fig. 6

fig. 7

Designed and pieced by Mary Balagna
Quilted by Ron and Kay Gerard

Won't You Be My Neighbor

A foundation-pieced neighborhood provides plenty of surprises and fun, with row after row of I-Spy windows that open and close. This quilt is dedicated to Mary's mom, Geraldine Bakunowicz.

FINISHED QUILT SIZE
36" x 53" (91.4 x 134.6 cm)

FINISHED BLOCK SIZE
6" x 7" (15.2 x 17.8 cm)

SEAM ALLOWANCE
¼" (6 mm)

MATERIALS
- Basic Supplies & Tools, page 11
- Foundation House Block Pattern, page 126
- **House:** 25 different fat eights or scraps, 6¼" x 7" (15.9 x 17.8 cm), of fabric
- **I-Spy windows:** 50 different novelty fussy-cut fabric scraps, 3" x 3" (7.6 x 7.6 cm)
- **Grass:** 25 green fabric scraps, at least 1½" x 7" (3.8 x 17.8 cm)
- **Roofs:** 25 different novelty scraps, at least 4" x 7" (10.2 x 17.8 cm)
- **Sky:** ½ yard (.5 m) of fabric
- **Window shutters:** 100 scraps of assorted tone-on-tone fabrics, each at least 3" x 3" (7.6 x 7.6 cm)
- **Borders and sashing:** 1½ yards (1.4 m) of fabric
- **Corner squares:** Fat eighth of contrasting fabric
- **Backing:** 2 yards (1.8 m) of backing fabric

- **Binding:** ⅔ yard (.6 m) of binding fabric
- **Batting:** 40" x 60" (101.6 x 152.4 cm), plus scraps for window shutters
- Paper for foundation piecing
- Glue stick

Notes: If you're piecing the vertical outer borders, you can use 1 yard (.9 m) of fabric. The backing for this quilt must be horizontally pieced.

Cutting

For each house (25 total), cut the pieces as follows. Pieces are cut slightly larger than necessary, to make sure that they adequately cover the assigned area for foundation piecing.

From the house fabric scraps:
Cut one 1½" x 2¾" (3.8 x 7 cm) rectangle (piece #1).

Cut two 1¾" x 2¾" (4.4 x 7 cm) rectangles (pieces #4 and #5).

Cut two 1½" x 7" (3.8 x 17.8 cm) rectangles (pieces #6 and #8).

From the I-Spy items window fabric:
Cut two 2¼" x 2¾" (5.7 x 7 cm) (pieces #2 and #3).

From the grass fabric:
Cut one 1¼" x 7" (3.2 x 17.8 cm)

rectangle (piece #7).

From the roof fabric:
Cut one 3¼" x 6¾" (8.3 x 17.1 cm) rectangle (piece #9).

From the sky fabric:
Cut two 4" x 5½" (10.2 x 14 cm) rectangles, cut in half on the diagonal in opposite directions (piece #10 and #11); save your leftover triangles for the next block.

From the window shutter fabric:
Cut four 2⅛" x 2⅝" (5.4 x 6.7 cm) rectangles. You'll need two shutters per house, so 100 rectangles total.

From the batting:
Cut two 2⅛" x 2⅝" (5.4 x 6.7 cm) rectangles for the pair of window shutters.

From the border/sashing fabric:
Cut six strips, 3½" (8.9 cm) x WOF (width of fabric), for sashing and horizontal borders.

Cut four strips, 3½" (8.9 cm) x WOF, for the vertical borders.

From the corner squares fabric:
Cut four 3½" (8.9 cm) squares.

From the binding fabric:
Cut six strips, 2½" (6.4 cm) x WOF.

DIFFICULTY

To some, acts of service and compassion come naturally.

To others, they must be learned. The learning process can be lengthy, evolving over a lifetime, or it can come in an instant depending on the method by which we are taught. I wish I could say that identifying charitable opportunities always came naturally to me, but they didn't. I would like to think, however, that specific instances in my youth where I offered my help to others actually created my educational path toward a life where charity became my focus. Although I never really envisioned inviting everyone in and outside my world to become my neighbor, it really did happen.

My first taste of charitable service came when I was a freshman in high school. Each homeroom was challenged to collect food items to fill gift baskets that would then be given to needy families in our community. Every morning, each of us felt a sense of pleasure and accomplishment as we witnessed the literal fruits of our generosity fill not one, but three baskets to overflowing. On the final day of the collection, our teacher applauded us for our efforts and asked for volunteers to deliver the baskets to the recipient families. The room was silent. No one volunteered. It seemed each student, including myself, was happy to collect and donate food items, but actually making the physical connection between our acts of service and a family in need of our compassion and love did not come naturally to us.

That afternoon during my ride home from school, I told my mom that no one volunteered to deliver the baskets. She was astonished. Fortunately, she had the foresight to recognize this delivery as an important and meaningful opportunity, and she did not

Assembly

Creating the Blocks

1 To create the shutters, place two of the same color of shutter fabric rectangles, right sides together, on top of a 2⅛ x 2⅝-inch (5.4 x 6.7 cm) rectangle of batting. Sew around three sides, leaving a short end open.

2 Clip the corners and turn right side out. Topstitch close to the edge around three sides, leaving the top edge open. Repeat steps 1 and 2 to create all 50 shutters.

3 Photocopy or trace the Foundation House Block Pattern onto the foundation paper. Make 25 copies, one for each house block.

4 Using the cutting list as a guide for which color fabric to use, paper piece each house block in numerical order, following the Paper Piecing instructions on page 13. Insert a shutter over each window (pieces #2 and #3), and sew them into the seam when adding piece #8.

Assembling the Quilt Top

5 Join the blocks into five rows of five blocks each.

6 Measure the length of the rows and cut four sashing strips to size. Join the horizontal block rows together with these strips.

Note: Always measure the size of the finished blocks and adjust the length of the sashing strips accordingly, as needed.

---

want me to miss it. She told me that this was the best part of all, and insisted that I offer our help. Her excitement intrigued me. I wasn't sure why she felt that I needed to take on this task but looking back, that experience was life changing for me. As we loaded the baskets of food and goodies into the car, warm feelings of excitement were ignited in my heart. The baskets, filled to overflowing, were a sight to behold! We knocked on the door, it opened, and we were invited inside a very humble home. I will never forget the feelings of love and gratitude that each family member expressed to us, feelings that transcended our language barrier. What a momentous occasion for me as I learned in an instant what it meant to serve others and to be a neighbor in every sense of the word.

Since that time, I found that it has become much easier to identify opportunities to help others, although I still have much to learn. As a quilter, I have always felt that the hug of a handmade quilt can help to heal the bodies and souls of those going through a crisis. My husband, an emergency room physician, would relate stories of children rushed to the hospital who were not only suffering physically but were also experiencing feelings

of anguish and fear as they entered an environment that was totally foreign and frightening to them. After thinking about how I could help, the thought came to mind that each of these children needed their very own quilt! So, I began to make quilts for him to give to his young patients. One day, I was watching my favorite television show, "Simply Quilts." The host of the show, Alex Anderson, was interviewing Karen Loucks-Baker. Karen was the founder of an organization called Project Linus. She explained that Project Linus chapters donated handmade blankets as gifts to seriously ill and traumatized children. I couldn't contain my excitement! This was exactly what I was doing, yet on a much larger scale and with the most perfect name! I have ALWAYS loved Linus, and I wanted to be a part of Project Linus as a chapter coordinator. With the help of others, I knew I could offer comfort and security to many more children in our area as part of this national organization. In January of 1999, the Project Linus Central Illinois Chapter officially opened and began to grow.

In 2000, the second annual Project Linus National Conference was held in Denver, Colorado. My daughter, Cari, and I

(Continued on p. 117)

Adding Borders

7 Add borders following the Adding a Border with Corner Squares instructions, page 14.

Finishing the Quilt

8 Create the backing, following the instructions on page 15. Layer the backing, batting, and quilt top to make a quilt sandwich and baste the layers together.

9 Quilt as desired.

10 Sew the binding strips together and bind the edge of the quilt, following the Binding instructions, page 17.

(Continued from p. 115)

decided to attend, and although we didn't know any of the other attendees, as soon as we walked in the door, we felt welcome. While in the hotel elevator, Cari and I met Carol Babbitt and her husband, Kirk. Carol was the chapter coordinator from Minneapolis/St. Paul, Minnesota, and we immediately became friends. We had no idea how Project Linus would guide our friendship at the time, but looking back we couldn't be happier with the path we have taken.

In September 2000, just a few months after conference, I received a letter from Project Linus National Headquarters. As I read through the letter my heart sank. In a nutshell, it stated that after much thought and discussion, the Board of Directors had decided to close the organization. I was devastated. I immediately went to our Project Linus online discussion group for support. None of us wanted this to happen, and many felt that it would be best to continue our mission as independent organizations. I bought a book, talked with a lawyer, and began the paperwork to open my own non-profit organization with the same mission of offering comfort and security to children through the gift of a handmade blanket. On October 27, 2000, Project Linus Central Illinois became official. Later on the same day, I received a call from Carol Babbitt who was thrilled to tell me that Project Linus was not closing, that she was the new national president, and that she would like me to be the vice-president. Unfortunately, my response did not convey the same excitement. It had nothing to do with Carol; she was a very capable businesswoman, a tremendous chapter coordinator, and a good friend. I was simply afraid of the unknown. Would this work? Would anyone join with us? Would I have the time? Would my family support me? Within a few days, I discovered the answer to each question would be a resounding YES and Project Linus was reborn! My neighborhood expanded once again from my Central Illinois Chapter to hundreds of chapters across the country, served by thousands of kind, generous, and skilled "blanketeers."

Donating blankets to seriously ill and traumatized children became a priority in my life. With faith and family ranking first and second on my list, Project Linus placed a close third. Throughout the years, my husband and each of my four children became a part of the Project Linus neighborhood through their service to the organization. Although I had delivered thousands of blankets to children in crisis, I was fortunate that my own family had not experienced the trauma or heartache that I witnessed time and time again. Then, on February 7th, 2006 that changed. A tragedy unlike any other knocked at our door. My daughter Cari and her twin boys, Luke and Logan, were visiting from Arizona. At 2 and a half years old, Luke and Logan were very healthy, active little boys, and as our first grandchildren, we cherished every moment with them. On that particular evening while the boys were playing, Luke collapsed without any warning. I called 911 while my husband tried to revive him. He remained unresponsive in spite of all of his "Papa's" efforts and passed away a few hours later. Luke's heart stopped due to an undiagnosed heart condition called "Prolonged QT," which can cause a heart arrhythmia and sudden death in those affected. In the weeks to follow, several members of our family were diagnosed with the same condition, and within 3 months, our son Alex and grandson Logan had surgery to implant internal defibrillators. These devices would serve to restart their hearts if such a situation would occur. While in the hospital, both Alex and Logan received Project Linus blankets. Not only did the quilts serve to comfort them while they were recovering from surgery, but we all felt the compassion and love that went into the creation of these hugs of comfort by kind and generous Project Linus blanketeers. My transformation from a chapter coordinator donating and delivering blankets to the parent and grandparent of a blanket recipient is something that has increased my dedication and devotion to Project Linus.

I have also discovered that the emotional and spiritual healing following a crisis is a "forever process" which is accomplished in a variety of ways. I decided to create a quilt as a reminder of our neighbors. A neighbor is not only defined as a person who lives near another but also someone who shows kindness or helpfulness toward his other fellow human beings. Project Linus has helped me to identify my neighbors and to BE a neighbor. It has transformed my life into a life of service where I instinctively ask the question "Won't You Be My Neighbor?" each every time the opportunity presents itself.

Mary Balagna

Templates

Enlarge templates to the percentages provided

Pretty Pockets

Pocket Template (150%)

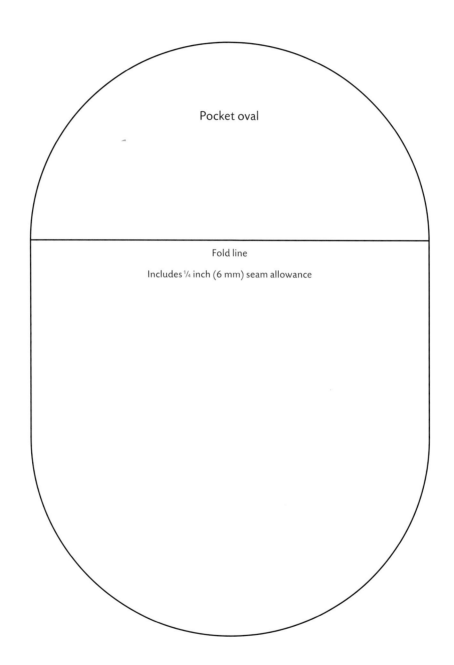

Pocket oval

Fold line

Includes ¼ inch (6 mm) seam allowance

Pocket Full of Posies
(150%)

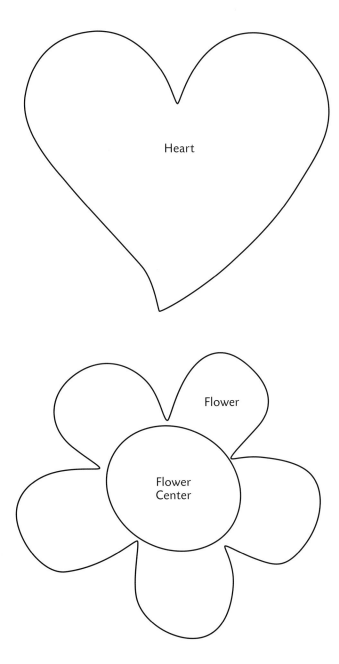

Heart

Flower

Flower
Center

Turtles Hiding in the Marsh

Includes ¼ inch (6 mm) seam allowance

(150%)

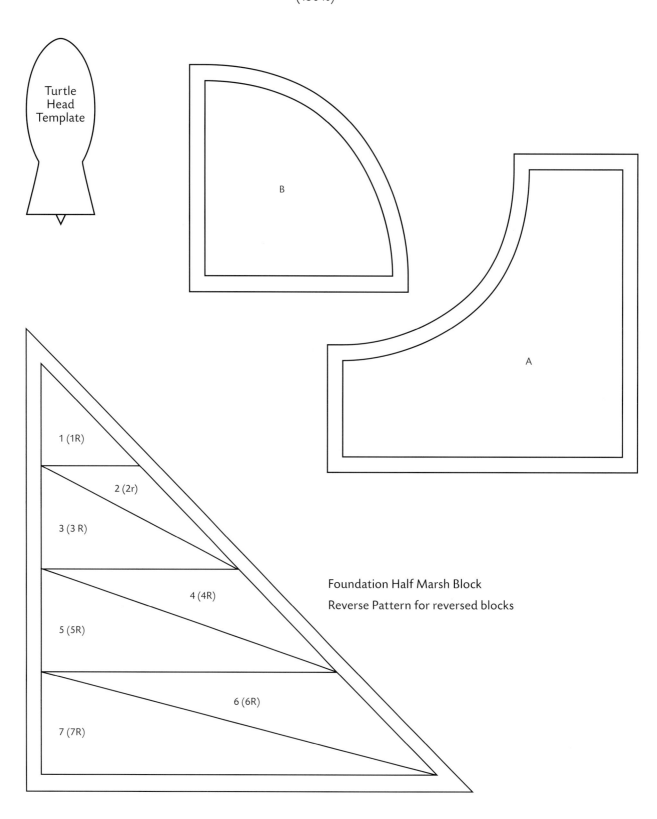

Turtle
Head
Template

B

A

1 (1R)

2 (2r)

3 (3 R)

4 (4R)

5 (5R)

6 (6R)

7 (7R)

Foundation Half Marsh Block

Reverse Pattern for reversed blocks

Sweet Simplicity

Toy Templates (200%)

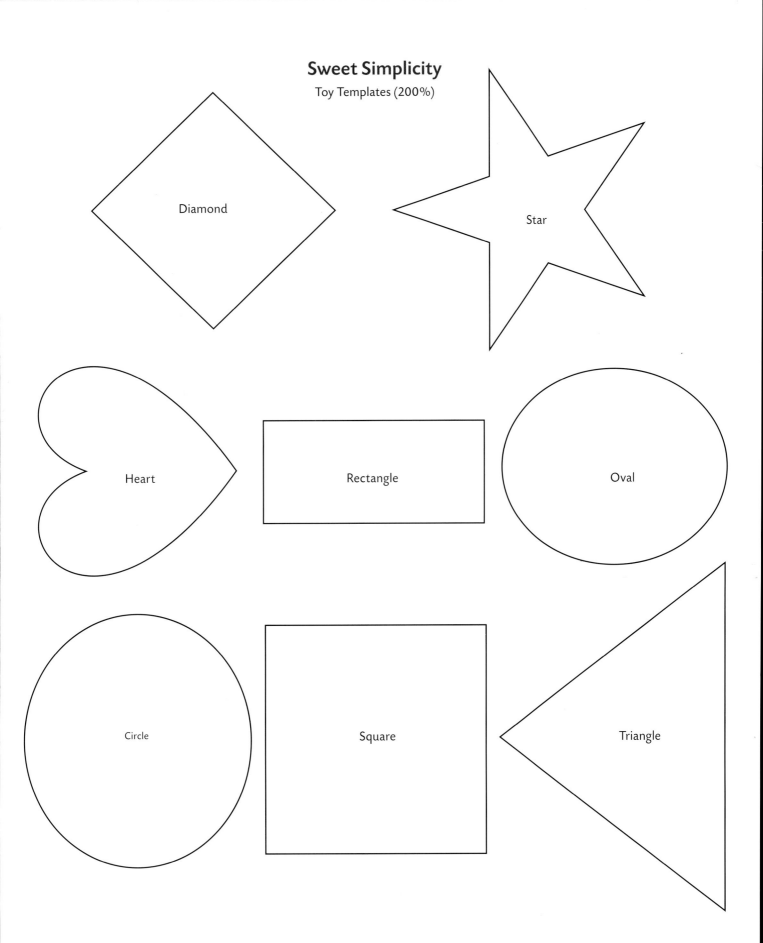

Diamond

Star

Heart

Rectangle

Oval

Circle

Square

Triangle

Covered in Love

Foundation Heart Block Pattern (175%)

Includes ¼ inch (6 mm) seam allowance

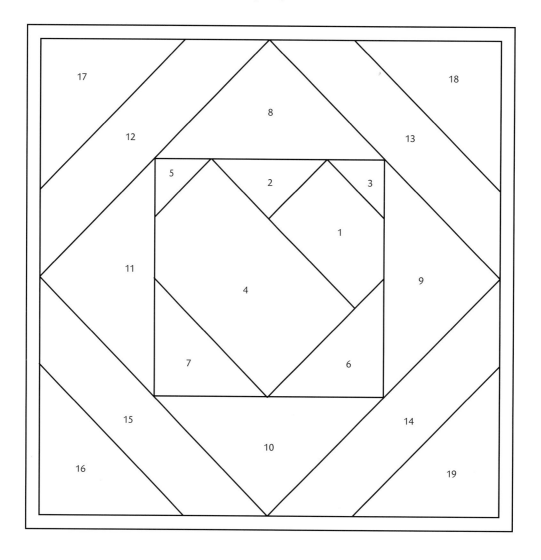

Handling It Together
Foundation Bar Block Pattern (150%)
Includes ¼ inch (6 mm) seam allowance

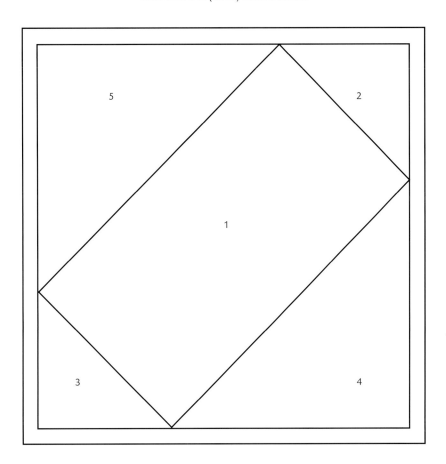

Channer's Checkers (200%)

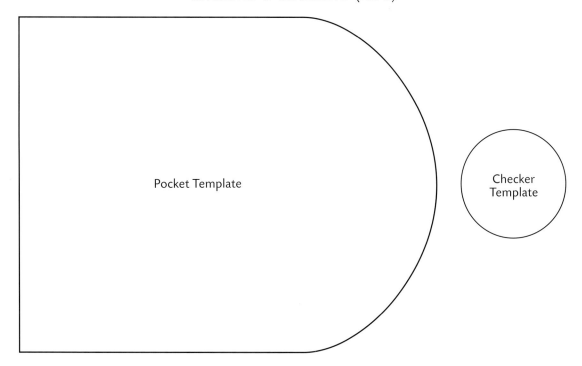

Pocket Template

Checker Template

EIEIO
(200%)

Duck

Cow

Horse

Pig

Sheep

Rooster

Remember Who You Are

(200%)

Won't You Be My Neighbor

Foundation House Block Pattern (100%)

Includes ¼ inch (6 mm) seam allowance

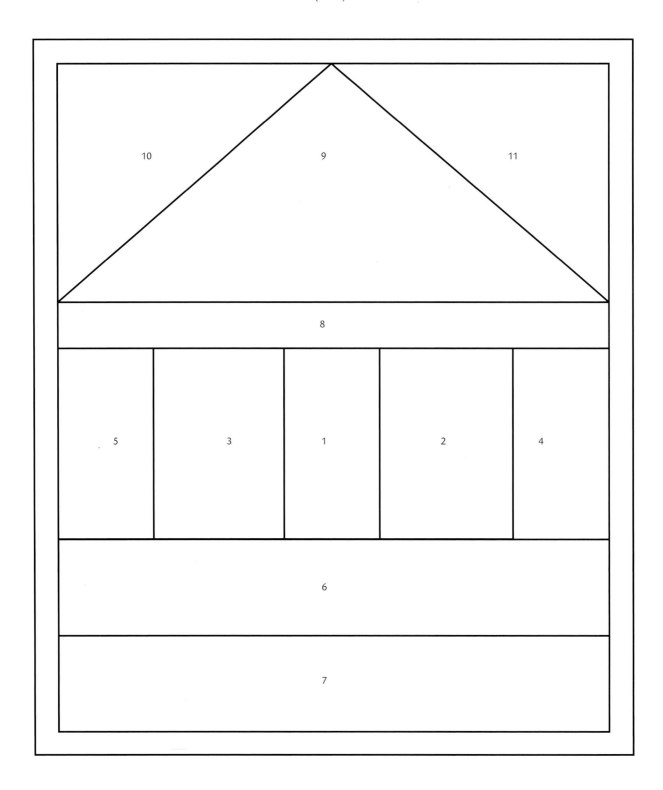

About the Authors

Carol Babbitt is the National President and Executive Director of Project Linus, headquartered in Bloomington, Illinois. She has a deep-seated love for all things domestic, including quilting and sewing of all kinds. In addition, she loves to crochet, cross-stitch, paint, cook, bake, and do just about anything artsy and crafty. Her first experience with a sewing machine was in 4-H as a 10 year old. She found she had an interest in textile art while in college, which translated into a love of quilting later on. While happy as a stay-at-home mom raising two boys, Carol chanced upon an article about Project Linus and her life was changed forever. She now resides in Bloomington, Illinois, where she works full-time taking care of Project Linus, two dogs, one cat, and her husband, who makes the things that are important to her, important to him.

Mary Balagna is the National Vice-President of Project Linus. As a University of Iowa graduate of the College of Pharmacy, she enjoyed working in the health care field for several years while developing her interest in quilts and quilting. In order to be a stay-at-home mom, she left the workforce and then eventually became acquainted with Project Linus. Her fascination—or as some may say obsession—with fabric and quilting led her to a full-time volunteer position as the Central Illinois Chapter Coordinator and National Vice-President of the organization. Although she is still "technically" considered a pharmacist, her role has evolved from dispensing medication in a drug store to dispensing blankets to children in crisis. Project Linus has been a major part of the lives of her husband and best friend, Terry, and each of her four children throughout the years. Her children have since married and blessed her with eight beautiful grandchildren (so far!), all potential Project Linus volunteers!

Acknowledgments

A special thanks to the following people who shared their creative and inspired designs:

Judy Brumaster	Caroline Embleton	Shirley Hughes	Merlene Sanborn
Elzora Channer	Kim Hazlett	Patricia Hickey	Cari Shields
	Cheryl Hughes	Ernestine Mrozinski	

We'd also like to thank the following models:

Gwendolyn Alvarado	Katrina Collins	Sophia Hanna	Zen Wissler
Luke Collins	Marley Curtis	Faith Medina	Ravi Wissler
	Isabella Hanna	Bodhi Wissler	

Index

Love crafting for charity?